GOURMET
SOAPS
MADE EASY

GOURMET
SOAPS
MADE EASY

MELINDA COSS

NEW
HOLLAND

For 'Railea', who blows great bubbles.

First published in 2001 by
New Holland Publishers (UK) Ltd
London • Cape Town • Sydney • Auckland

Garfield House
86-88 Edgware Road
London W2 2EA
United Kingdom
www.newhollandpublishers.com

80 McKenzie Street
Cape Town 8001
South Africa

Level 1, Unit 4, 14 Aquatic Drive
Frenchs Forest, NSW 2086
Australia

218 Lake Road
Northcote, Auckland
New Zealand

10 9 8 7 6 5 4 3 2 1

ISBN 1 85974 626 8 (HB)
ISBN 1 85974 995 X (PB)

Senior Editor: Clare Hubbard
Editorial Assistant: Paul McNally
Design: Design Revolution
Photographer: Emma Peios
Stylist: Blackjacks
Production: Hazel Kirkman

Editorial Direction: Rosemary Wilkinson

Reproduction by Modern Age Repro House Ltd, Hong Kong
Printed and bound in Singapore by Tien Wah Press (Pte) Ltd

Acknowledgements

As my publishers are more than aware, this book is a triumph over adversity. Fire, flood, illness and the loss of a very dear brother all descended on me in its formative months whilst, at the same time, I had the responsibility of expanding my little 'The Handmade Soap Company' from a kitchen-sink operation into a grown-up, international business now making soaps for the high street multiples. For this reason I give very special thanks to my editors, Rosemary Wilkinson and Clare Hubbard, and apologies to Yvonne McFarlane who, on at least two occasions, received desperate snivelling emails from me saying 'I just can't do this!'. With calm patience, I was persuaded that 'I could' and it seems that I did. I am equally grateful for the extraordinary eye of Emma Peios who has, yet again, transformed my soaps into works of art with her magic camera. Thanks also to all my colleague soapmakers on the internet who so generously share new information. Last, but not least, thanks to the team at 'The Handmade Soap Company' for their unfailing support.

Note

To give you the option of working in either ounces or grams, it has been necessary to round up or down the conversion figures slightly. These small differences will not affect your end result. Use either ounces or grams, but do not mix the two in a recipe.

Disclaimer

The information in this book has been carefully researched and all efforts have been made to ensure accuracy. The author and publisher assume no responsibility for any injuries, damages or losses incurred either during, or subsequent to, following the instructions in this book.

Contents

Introduction   6

Soapy facts   8

Materials and equipment   12

Oils and additives   15

Making scents   20

Colouring   24

Meltdown   26

Basic instructions   27

Soap en-croûte   28

RECIPES

Cocktails   32

Appetizers   39

Herb and nut pâtés   46

Salads   52

Patisserie   58

Petit fours   67

A la carte   72

The soap biz   77

Stockists and resources   79

Index   80

Introduction

It's quite amazing how much thought is required in making a bar of soap. Soap can be moulded, stamped, decorated and wrapped, all of which allow you, the maker, to express your creative spirit. Not only will you have the pleasure of wonderful scents as you work, soapmaking will also provide you with a never-ending palette of colours and textures with which to create your designs.

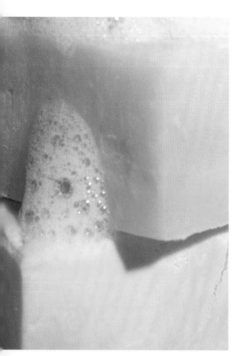

For those of you who love cookery, here is an art that requires all your culinary skills. The chances are that you already have all the equipment you need in your kitchen cupboard so no great expense is involved either. Soapmaking also has the added advantage of keeping your waistline intact – you can sample the finished product to your heart's delight and do yourself nothing but good.

For the health conscious and the environmentalist, soapmaking offers the opportunity to control what goes on your skin and to abandon all the detergent bars that are currently presented to us as 'soap'. The recipes in this book contain no artificial preservatives and give you the choice of using manmade cosmetic pigments and fragrances or natural colourants and essential oils. It is more than possible to make a wonderful bar of soap with completely natural ingredients that will not deteriorate over time.

If you have a passion for alchemy, you are in for a treat. This is a highly unpredictable art and the chemist in you will spend hours, if not weeks, trying to fathom strange shapes, absurd colour changes and unexpected textures. You will learn, as I have, that a recipe made on a wet Monday will look completely different if repeated on a dry Tuesday. Do not strive for perfection but enjoy the unexpected. To say the experience is addictive is an understatement.

Soap is also one of the few crafts that is non-sexist and non-ageist. The only exception is that all soap is made with caustic soda and for this reason, cold-process soapmaking is not a hobby for unsupervised children. However, kids can really stretch their creativity as they play with a pot of melt and pour soap base together with some colours and fragrances. This method does not require the addition of caustic soda and I have included a selection of melt and pour recipes in this book to feed the imagination.

Since I wrote *The Handmade Soap Book* I have made many new discoveries and found better ways of doing certain things. For those who have that book, some of the information here may seem contradictory but soapmaking is a wonderful journey and you will learn as you make.

There are also now many fellow soapmakers with whom you can share your discoveries, most particularly on the internet. Check out my resource page for more information. There are email soap lists in the UK now as well as in the US so do join them.

Regrettably, soapmaking is not an instant path to a small, successful business. There is a considerable amount of legislation and financial investment involved in the selling of soap in Europe, and I have covered this on p77–78. Enjoy your soap, make it for gifts but please do not try to sell it until you have thoroughly researched all the legal requirements.

Happy Bubbles
Melinda

Soapy facts

'Soap' is the magical result of mixing an acid with a caustic alkali. Historically, the alkali (or lye) was made by dripping water through hardwood ashes. These days, most methods of soapmaking use sodium hydroxide (caustic soda) as the alkali, and vegetable or animal fats and oils as the acid. Caustic soda can be obtained from any hardware shop or do-it-yourself centre, but check that it is at least 95 per cent pure before you buy it.

Most oils and fats can be used as the acid but each requires a specific amount of alkali to turn it into soap (see Saponification chart, p19). The most crucial challenge to the soapmaker is ensuring the correct balance of ingredients for a fine soap that is neither caustic nor fatty and that contains the moisturizing, conditioning or foaming properties that you personally want to achieve in your soap. You will find information on how to select your oils on p15.

Water is the third crucial ingredient in soapmaking. Its main job is to dissolve the sodium hydroxide (caustic soda) so that it can, in turn, do its job converting the oils into soap. Whilst the amount of water you use is not crucial, approximately one part water to three parts fat will ensure the chemistry works and that the resulting bar is not too soft. The quality of the water you use is important. It needs to be soft and pure. Bottled distilled water is a good option and you can also use rainwater provided you run it through a filter to eliminate nature's debris.

As an alternative to water, many soapmakers prefer to use goat's milk. However, during the saponification process, the milk can curdle and turn a nasty yellow. It also makes the initial mix smell quite strongly of ammonia. Despite these problems, the use of goat's milk results in a wonderful creamy bar of soap and is well worth the initial problems. I have yet to have any success using cow's milk and my personal ideal is 50:50 water and goat's milk.

Saponification

When the alkali is diluted with liquid and added to the acid, a reaction called 'saponification' occurs. Once this has happened, the alkali is on its way to being neutralized and, after curing the soap for several weeks, it should no longer be in evidence. Soap, therefore, is 'made with' sodium hydroxide but does not 'contain' it.

Saponification is an easy stage to recognize but the time it takes depends on a large number of variables including the temperature of your mixture, the weather, the water content and your methods of mixing. The specific fats that you are using

(see Oils and additives, p15) also add to the equation. This is one of the wonderful imponderables involved in soapmaking and the lesson to be learnt is to always leave yourself plenty of time.

Trace

When saponification occurs, your soap thickens to a point referred to by soapmakers as 'trace'. To establish whether you have reached trace, spoon some soap from the pot and then dribble it back over the surface of the mixture. If the dribble sits on top of the mixture (forming a raised line), you have reached trace. Whilst trace can occur in as little time as five minutes, do not worry if it takes several hours. Unless you have made a big mistake with your weights and measures, the soap will trace eventually.

Colourings, fragrances and fillers are all added as the mixture reaches trace. The soap is then poured into moulds, covered with a blanket for insulation and left to set.

Weights and measures

The success or failure of your batch of soap relies on, above all, one crucial factor: correct proportions of ingredients. If you wish to add to or alter the ingredients, read the Saponification chart (see p19) for guidance on how to do this.

The majority of recipes in this book will give you approximately one kilogram (2lb) batches. Depending on the moulds you select, this should provide you with 10–14 average sized bars of soap.

Please note that with the exception of spoonfuls, drops and millilitres, all quantities listed in the recipes are weighed quantities. For example, where water is quoted in ounces, these are weighed ounces and not fluid ounces. Put the relevant empty container on the scales and turn the scales back to zero. Then add your ingredients to the container until the weight reads as specified. To give you the option of working in either grams or ounces, it has been necessary to slightly round up or down the conversion figure. These small differences will not

affect your end result. Do not use a combination of metric and imperial measurements – for accuracy, keep to one system.

Shortcuts

There are a number of ways that trace times can be reduced. Whisking the soap with a stainless steel whisk will speed up the procedure as will the use of a hand-held electric mixer. If, however, you are going to use one of these miracles of modern science, please ensure that you place it into the soap pot before switching it on.

Another shortcut is to place your soap pot in a warm oven (lowest setting), although personally, I find that with small batches the old fashioned look and stir approach is preferable as it ensures that you will not miss trace and find that your soap has solidified in the pot.

Setting times

These once again are dependent on a number of factors (ingredients, room temperature, etc) but, on average, your soap should be hard enough to remove from the mould 24–48 hours after pouring. Soaps based on olive and sunflower oils take longer to harden than those made with vegetable fats and it is important to take them out of the mould as soon as the soap reaches a 'hard cheese' consistency. At this stage, you will be able to cut it into bars with ease. Soaps made with animal fats are generally harder.

Curing

Once your soap is cut, stack it in a well ventilated room and cover it with blankets to continue the curing process. During this process, any residual sodium hydroxide (lye) is neutralized and this can result in changes to the appearance of your soap. The first thing

Left: Using bottled, distilled water will guarantee a soap's purity. Goat's milk can be used instead to make a beautifully creamy soap.

you may notice is that a fine white dust or even a crust appears on the surface of the soap. This is soda ash and it can be scraped or even washed off the soap once the curing process is completed. Some soapmakers find that soda ash formation can be limited by covering the surface of your soap with cling film directly after it has been poured into the mould. There is great debate as to how and why soda ash forms on some batches of soap and not on others. The argument continues, but in any event soda ash is easily removed.

You will also find that your soap will shrink during the curing process and, for this reason, it is wise not to attach paper bands until the soap has completely settled. Some colourings will also fade. To reduce this possibility, turn the soap regularly so that exposure to light is equal throughout the curing process.

In this book we use two methods of soapmaking: firstly 'the cold-process' method, which is a traditional technique that ensures that the glycerine – a valuable by-product of the saponification process – remains in the finished soap. This is often extracted in commercial soapmaking and sold separately. In fact, many commercial soaps are not soap at all but a combination of detergents, emulsifiers, surfactants and chemical preservatives.

Secondly, 'melt and pour' soaps are featured. These are made using a ready-made glycerine base and are very quick and easy to produce.

Many of you will be aware and concerned about the term 'pH balance'. This is a term used to measure acidity. Most cold-process soaps have a 'pH balance' of around 9–10, but soapers aim to reduce this to 7 or 8 (just above neutral). The pH of your soap will reduce during the curing process but it is hard to control without using harsh chemicals and these are, in effect, worse for your skin than a soap with a high pH.

Left: You can use litmus paper to test the pH balance of your soap. Soap tends to be alkaline, but this can be reduced by the addition of acid.

The addition, at trace, of diluted citric acid or vinegar will help reduce the pH but establishing correct quantities is purely a matter of trial and error. An easier solution is to 'superfat' your soap by adding up to 5 per cent more fat (or less sodium hydroxide) than the amount strictly required for saponification. Whilst the ingredients of the soaps in this book ensure they are mild and gentle, if you are concerned you can test the pH of your soap with papers that can be purchased from aquarium shops, school suppliers or chemical laboratories. If a soap reads above 10, don't throw it away, use it for the laundry or re-batch it (see p26).

Troubleshooting

As I have said before, soapmaking is not a precise art and, whilst all the included recipes have been tried and tested, you may experience some unexpected reactions. Nine times out of ten, failed batches are due to inaccurate measuring of the ingredients. This is easily done, so when preparing batches do give the matter at hand your full attention.

Below is a list of common problems and suggestions as to how you should deal with them.

1. Curdling: If you have ever poured sour milk into your tea you will have a good idea of the visual appearance of 'curdling'. This is quite common in soaps containing milk and these can successfully be whisked into a smooth mixture. Use an electric whisk to do this and work quickly. Be prepared to pour the soap quite quickly as trace will speed up considerably. Curdling sometimes occurs when you mix the fats and sodium hydroxide (lye) at a very high temperature.

2. Seizing: If your soap mixture appears to be setting in the pan it is often due to a reaction caused by the fragrance or essential oils. Pour the soap (or spoon it) immediately into your mould and do your best to flatten the surface. Your basic soap should be fine to use, just not as pretty as it should be.

3. Crumbly soap: This can be caused by too little water. Your final soap will be difficult to cut without breaking and could prove to be quite harsh. Your choice here is to re-batch the soap (see p26) or to grate it and use it as laundry soap.

4. Separation: This becomes apparent after you have poured your soap into the mould. A significant layer of oil or grease sits on the top of the mixture. If the layer of oil is only

thin, it is probably caused by the essential oils and will be re-absorbed during the curing process. If the layer is thick, you have a caustic soap that should be discarded. This has probably been caused by an excess of sodium hydroxide (lye) in the initial mixture.

5. No trace: Your soap can take hours and hours to reach trace so, if you are sure your ingredients were weighed correctly, don't worry about it. Leave it as long as you can, stirring frequently and then pour it into the mould. It will trace eventually.

6. Soft soap after several days: Some combinations of oils (particularly sunflower and olive) seem to take a lifetime to harden. An excess of water can also prolong the time it takes the soap to harden or you may have included too little sodium hydroxide (lye). Leave the soap in the mould, if it hardens eventually, it should be all right to use.

7. Small white chunks in soap: These are caused by an excess of sodium hydroxide (lye) or inadequate stirring. The white areas are caustic and the soap should be discarded.

8. Small bubbles of liquid trapped in hard soap: Again, this is caused by excessive amounts of sodium hydroxide (lye) or inadequate stirring. The liquid in the bubbles is caustic, discard the soap.

9. Soap has turned to jelly: This looks like a big problem but some soapmakers prefer their soap to reach this 'gel stage' as it does result in a harder bar of soap. The cause is not clear but I suspect it is related to overheating, which can happen as a reaction to some essential and fragrance oils. It also tends to happen more frequently when you are making large batches of soap.

10. Soap will not release from mould: Put it in the freezer for an hour or so and try again. If you forgot to grease your mould this can cause the problem but freezing certainly helps.

11. White powder forms on the surface of the soap: This is very common and quite harmless. Scrape or wash the powder off the soap before wrapping it. The problem can be reduced by placing cling film directly on the surface of the soap after it has been poured into the mould.

Materials and equipment

Most of the equipment that you need to begin cold-process soapmaking is already in your kitchen cupboard. You need even less for the melt and pour method. Provided you wash this equipment after soapmaking in normal dishwashing liquid, there is no need to set aside special pots, pans and utensils specifically for your new addiction.

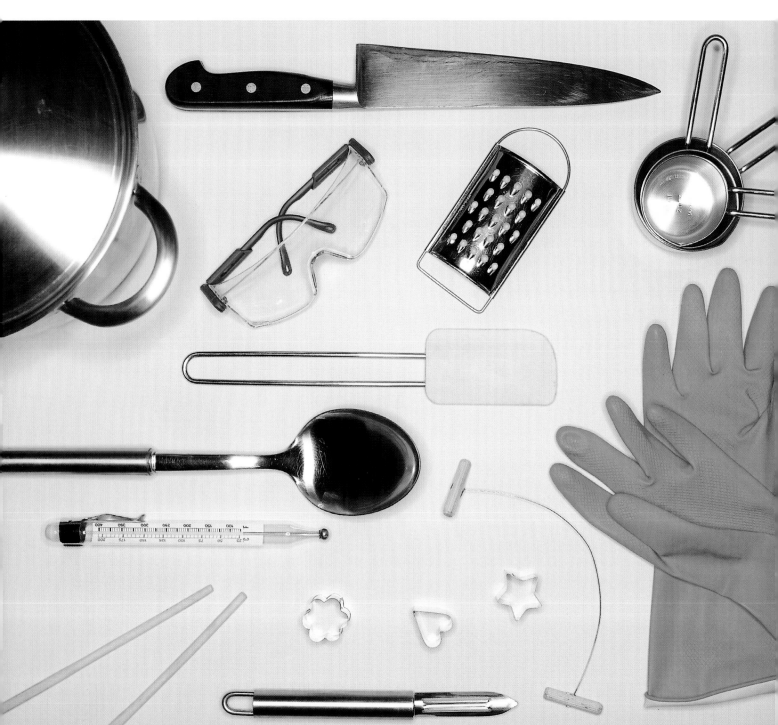

Check that you have the following:

One large cooking pot
This is your soap pot and should be made of either stainless steel or unchipped enamel. Do not use iron or aluminium as these will be affected by the lye (caustic soda). A double boiler is useful for melt and pour soap but not essential, and this does not need to be stainless steel.

Plastic or ovenproof glass measuring jug or bowl
This will be used for weighing your water and for mixing your sodium hydroxide (lye). When making melt and pour soap, you place your soap base in this and stand it in your large cooking pot.

Two plastic spatulas
These are for stirring your soap mix and your sodium hydroxide (lye), and also for scraping the sides of your soap pot. You can use wooden spoons but they will perish in time.

Stainless steel ladle
When making large batches of soap, you may find it easier to ladle rather than pour the mixture into the moulds.

Sugar thermometers
You will need two for the cold-process method and one for melt and pour. Buy glass thermometers rather than aluminium, and ensure that they register from below 38°C (100°F) and up to at least 93°C (200°F).

Kitchen scales
Normal kitchen scales will do fine (providing they are accurate) but if you are buying new ones invest in scales you can manually turn back to zero. Postage scales are particularly useful for measuring the sodium hydroxide (lye). If you plan to sell your soap you will need 'stamped for trade' registered scales (see The Soap Biz, p77).

Moulds
Assorted plastic containers to use as moulds (see Moulds, p14).

Non-stick cooking spray
This is used for greasing your moulds. If you don't have any, solid vegetable fat (cold-process only) can be used.

Sharp knife or cheese wire
For cutting soap into bars.

Potato peeler or cheese slicer
To use for trimming soap.

Rubber gloves
To protect your hands, especially when handling sodium hydroxide (lye).

Eye protection
Always use a large pair of spectacles or plastic protective goggles. These can be bought in most DIY stores (cold-process only).

Old blankets or towels
To insulate your finished soap (cold-process only).

Cheese grater or food processor
You will need a hand-held cheese grater or food processor for re-batching (cold-process only).

Sponges or dishcloths
For mopping up spilt soap.

Sodium hydroxide (caustic soda/lye)
This can be purchased from DIY shops, chemists or plumber's supply merchants. Be sure the brand you buy contains at least 95 per cent sodium hydroxide. Keep this in an airtight container and handle with extreme care. If the granules are exposed to damp, they will solidify into hard lumps (cold-process only).

Dropper (optional)
For adding diluted pigments.

Measuring spoons and jugs
Assorted measuring spoons and small jugs to use for colourants and additives.

Wooden chopsticks, kebab skewers or toothpicks
For swirling colours.

Vinegar
In case of accidents. This will neutralize the sodium hydroxide (cold-process only).

Cling film
For covering your newly poured soap.

Moulds

Your soap can be made in all shapes and sizes and before long you will find yourself collecting moulds from all sorts of strange places.

If you are making melt and pour soaps, you can use moulds made from virtually anything. However, when making cold-process soaps, be careful to avoid metals (other than stainless steel) as your soap is still caustic when you pour it and this can cause the metal to corrode very badly.

There are numerous custom-made soap moulds on the market. Many will give you individual stylized shapes and others provide the opportunity to make a set of, for example, heart-shaped soaps. Some purpose-made wooden moulds have dividers that eliminate the need to cut your soap, others have drop down sides so you can remove the soap with ease.

A number of suppliers are listed in the back of this book but as a starting point, consider using the following:

1. Plastic food packaging (i.e. the clear trays that hold fruit, vegetables, meat or biscuits).
2. Plastic jelly moulds and ice cube trays for guest soaps.
3. Cardboard or wooden boxes lined with dustbin bag or cling film.
4. Drawer dividers.
5. Plastic food storage containers.
6. Sections of drain pipe or electric conduit.

You can also make your soap in flat slabs and cut it into shapes with a cookie cutter.

Safety first

There is no way of getting around it, cold-processed soaps are made with sodium hydroxide (caustic soda) and it's nasty stuff. Just a grain can badly burn the skin and taken internally, it can be lethal. However, all that is required is a little common sense, and if you obey the following rules no harm will befall you.

1. Store sodium hydroxide in a clearly marked, airtight container on a high shelf.

2. Always wear rubber gloves when handling sodium hydroxide, mixing soap and taking fresh soap out of the moulds.

3. Always add the sodium hydroxide to the water and not the other way around. Choking fumes will rise from the bowl

so always work in a well ventilated area and keep your face away from the fumes. Better still, wear a mask or cover your face with a scarf. Don't worry, these fumes only last a few moments.

4. Wear eye goggles or large glasses when handling or mixing sodium hydroxide.

5. Do not rub your eyes. If the worst happens, rinse your eyes thoroughly in cold running water and go straight to the nearest Accident and Emergency unit.

6. Do not leave soap mixture or (worse still) caustic solution, unattended or in the reach of children or pets.

7. When making soap, keep a bottle of vinegar next to the sink. If accidental splashes occur, immediately wash affected area with the vinegar and then rinse with water.

8. When cleaning your soap pot, let the mixture harden and then scrape the remains into a plastic bag, which should be sealed and put out with the rubbish. Add vinegar to your washing up water and wash utensils as normal (wearing a pair of rubber gloves) with dishwashing liquid.

Cutting soap

If you are making your soap in a slab, you can cut it with a cheese wire or a flat bladed kitchen knife. Score the surface first to determine the size of your bars before cutting right through. Keep your knife level as you cut, and then square up uneven edges or surfaces with a vegetable knife or peeler. You can also level off uneven surfaces with a cheese slicer.

Oils and additives

Oils are a combination of a number of different fatty acids, each of which adds particular properties to your soap. As an example, olive oil contains 63–81 per cent oleic acid, which conditions the skin. Palmitic acid (prevalent in palm oil) produces a hard bar of soap but a slow lather, whereas coconut oil contains a high proportion of lauric acid, which produces rich fluffy bubbles. A combination of these three oils will therefore result in a hard, conditioning bar of soap with a rich creamy lather. On the following page you will find a chart compiled by Kathy Miller with the help of a number of soapmakers who share information on the internet. She has broken down the percentages and qualities of fatty acids in a large range of oils. Once you are addicted, (and you will be), this chart will help you to design your own, perfectly formed soap.

Superfatting

There are occasions when you may want small quantities of very precious oils to remain in your soap without being saponified. As a rule of thumb, you can safely add 5 per cent of extra oils without fear of rancidity. This can be calculated in several ways. One method is to add your precious oil after the soap has traced. Alternatively, you can add the oil to your base oils or you can calculate the sodium hydroxide for the whole batch (including the precious oil), and then discount the amount by 5 per cent. When superfatting, it is wise to incorporate a small amount of vitamin E oil or benzoin, both of which act as natural preservatives.

Additives

In addition to precious oils, there are a number of additives that will change the texture and various properties of your soap. When adding fresh herbs or fruits and vegetables, soak them in glycerine for at least 24 hours before use, and add 5ml (1tsp) of vitamin E oil per 454g (1lb) batch of soap. This will help to preserve them. As an alternative to vitamin E, add 5ml (1tsp) of grapefruit seed extract, carrot root oil, wheatgerm oil or benzoin to your soap mix. These are all natural preservatives.

Here are a few more fun ingredients to play around with:

Almonds (ground): Ground almonds are great for unplugging pores and exfoliating the skin. Only 5ml (1tsp) per 454g (1lb) of soap is required to leave your skin silky soft and free from oil. Be aware that some people are allergic to nuts.

Aloe vera gel: Extracted from the leaf of a cactus, this is a healing gel that is good for dry or chapped skin, eczema and for soothing burns.

Apricots: Dried or fresh apricots can be pulped and added to your soap. Apricots are packed with vitamins and minerals and serve as a valuable skin softener. Apricot kernel oil contains skin-softening properties, vitamins and minerals.

Beeswax: Available in white or gold and used widely as an emulsifier. Gives soap a lovely waxy feel and honey smell. It will add to the hardness of a bar and the speed of trace. Use 28g (1oz) per 454g (1lb) of soap.

Benzoin: Available in powder or liquid form. Benzoin is a natural preservative that also serves as a fixative for your fragrances.

Borax: This mineral increases the cleaning power of your soap, softens the water and also acts as a valuable disinfectant. Use only 5ml (1tsp) of borax powder per 454g (1lb) of soap. If you use more than this, you may have problems with the texture of your soap.

Bran: This is the outer husk of any grain and will add bulk and texture to your soap. It acts as a natural exfoliant as it is slightly abrasive. Add around 30ml (2tbsp) per 454g (1lb) of soap.

Carrots: Also available as an essential oil, carrots can be liquidized and added directly to soap. Rich in vitamins C and A,

Properties of oils

FATTY ACIDS:	Lauric	Linoleic	Myristic	Oleic	Palmitic	Ricinoleic	Stearic	Iodine
PROPERTIES:	hard bar cleansing fluffy lather	conditioning	hard bar cleansing fluffy lather	conditioning	hard bar stable lather	conditioning fluffy, stable lather	hard bar stable lather	lower numbers mean harder bar
OILS:								
Almond (sweet)		8–28%		64–82%	6–8%			93–106
Apricot kernel		20–34%		58–74%	4–7%			92–108
Avocado		6–18%		36–80%	7–32%		1.5%	80–95
Castor		3–4%		3–4%		90%		82–90
Cocoa butter		3%		34–36%	25–30%		31–35%	33–42
Coconut	39–54%	1–2%	15–23%	4–11%	6–11%		1–4%	<10
Canola		15%		32%	1%			105–120
Corn		45–56%		28–37%	12–14%		2–3%	103–130
Cottonseed		52%		18%	13%		13%	80
Emu oil		14%	0.4%	50%	21%		9%	75
Flax/linseed		7–19%		14–39%	4–9%		2–4%	105–115
Grapeseed		58–78%		12–28%	5–11%		3–6%	125–142
Hazelnut		7–11%		65–85%	4–6%		1–4%	90–103
Hemp oil		57%		12%	6%		2%	166.5
Jojoba				10–13%				80–85
Kukui nut		42%		20%	6%			155–175
Lard		6%	1%	46%	28%		13%	43–45
Macadamia		1–3%		54–63%	7–10%		2–6%	73–79
Mango		1–13%		34–56%	3–18%		26–57%	55–65
Olive		5–15%		63–81%	7–14%		3–5%	79–95
Palm		9–11%		38–40%	43–45%		4–5%	45–57
Palm kernel	47%		14%	18%	9%			37
Peach kernel		15–35%		55–75%	5–8%			108–118
Rice bran		32–47%		32–38%	13–23%		2–3%	105–115
Safflower		70–80%		10–20%	6–7%			86–119
Sesame		39–47%		37–42%	8–11%		4–6%	105–115
Shea butter		3–8%		40–55%	3–7%		35–45%	55–71
Soybean		46–53%		21–27%	9–12%		4–6%	124–132
Sunflower		70%		16%	7%		4%	119–138
Tallow		2–3%	3–6%	37–43%	24–32%		20–25%	43–45
Wheatgerm		55–60%		13–21%	13–20%		2%	125–135

For more technical information, I recommend a visit to Kathy's web site at: http://users.silverlink.net/~timer/soapdesign.html

carrots are particularly good for chapped and dry skin. They will also colour your soap orange.

Clay (French): Also known as 'bentonite', this is available in pink, white, red, grey, yellow and green. It is useful for drawing toxins and dirt from the skin and gives your soap a nice smooth finish. Not recommended for dry skin. Use approximately 15ml (1tbsp) per 454g (1lb) of soap and add an extra 100ml (3$\frac{1}{2}$fl oz) of water to your soap mix. Kaolin and Fullers Earth can be used for the same purpose. Mix your essential or fragrance oils with 5ml (1tsp) of clay before adding them to the soap mix. This will help suspend the fragrances in the soap and make them hold better.

Coffee: Fresh coffee beans, ground to a fine powder, are particularly useful for removing odours such as onion and garlic from your hands. Use approximately 50g (1$\frac{3}{4}$oz) brewed coffee grounds per 454g (1lb) of soap.

Cornmeal: In addition to adding bulk to your batch, cornmeal is a useful exfoliant for greasy skin. It is available in both yellow and white. Add 15ml (1tbsp) per 454g (1lb) of soap.

Cucumber: Often used in face packs, cucumbers have an astringent quality and good cleansing power. They should be liquidized and preserved with 5ml (1tsp) of vitamin E oil per 454g (1lb) of soap.

Flower petals: Dried flower petals can be ground up and added to your soap at 'trace'. Rose and lavender both have astringent qualities, whilst calendula (pot marigold) is good for rough or cracked skin. Ground petals (with the exception of calendula) will discolour in soap but when used with an appropriate essential oil they act as a desirable additive and produce a speckled effect. Use approximately 30ml (2tbsp) per 454g (1lb) of soap.

Evening primrose oil: Good for eczema and helps to prevent premature ageing of the skin.

Glycerine: A clear syrupy liquid produced naturally in cold-process soapmaking. Extra glycerine can be added to increase the moisturizing properties of the soap.

Grapefruit seed extract (GSE): A valuable antioxidant with antibacterial and deodorizing properties. Add 5ml (1tsp) to a 1kg (2lb) batch of oils to help speed up trace times.

Hazelnuts (ground): See almonds.

Herbs (dried): Herbs should be added at a ratio of 30ml (2tbsp) per 454g (1lb) of soap. Dried herbs not only add texture and a decorative 'country feel' to the finished soap, but they also have their own individual skincare properties. You can also infuse fresh herbs in your base oil where they will provide a natural fragrance.

Honey: Honey has wonderful emollient properties but for best results warm it before adding it to your soap mix and be sure to stir well. Use honey with beeswax or shea butter as it does have a tendency to soften soap.

Jojoba oil: Great in shampoo bars, jojoba oil is both a moisturizer and a humectant.

Lanolin: A wax that comes from sheep's wool, lanolin has great skin softening properties. Be aware though, that some people are allergic to lanolin.

Lemons and oranges: The dried and finely grated peel of citrus fruits contains a high level of vitamin C, which makes it a valuable additive in soapmaking. Lemons in particular have strong antibacterial qualities. However, the essential oils of the same fruits are notoriously difficult to use in soapmaking and seldom retain their scent. Use approximately 15ml (1tbsp) of powdered peel per 454g (1lb) of soap. Lemon juice can also be used as a part substitute for water.

Mustard powder: A small quantity of mustard powder can be added to soaps to help unclog pores.

Oatmeal: This will add pleasing texture to your soap and act as a gentle exfoliant. Use baby oatmeal or rolled oats ground with a food processor. Add approximately 50g (1$\frac{3}{4}$oz) oats per 454g (1lb) of soap for maximum mileage.

Pumice: The abrasive quality of finely ground pumice will help to remove stubborn dirt and stains from the hands. Add approximately 30ml (2tbsp) to every 454g (1lb) of soap. If you want to make your own pumice stones, add 113g (4oz) of pumice to 227g (8oz) of soap mixture, stir thoroughly and then quickly pour the mixture into greased moulds to set.

Seaweed: The use of seaweed improves the skin's texture and colour. Seaweed can be bought in powdered form from health food stores and also as a liquid extract. Seaweed is packed with vitamins and minerals but sadly, it is doubtful that these survive the saponification process. However, seaweed is well worth using for both its therapeutic and decorative qualities.

Shea butter: This makes a hard, creamy and conditioning soap bar – a truly luscious ingredient.

Silk fibres: These really do make your soap silky. Add a pinch of raw fibres to your caustic solution and stir. Continue making your soap in the normal way.

Spices: Powdered spices such as cinnamon, paprika and turmeric can be used in soap purely as natural colouring agents (see Colouring, p24). Whilst cloves have valuable antiseptic qualities, they can be irritating and should be avoided when soap is destined for use on sensitive skin.

Vitamin E oil: This is an antioxidant that retards deterioration of fresh matter in soap and also helps to prevent wrinkles.

Wheatgerm: This has many beneficial uses in soap. The germ itself can be powdered and used for its mildly abrasive quality. Add approximately 15ml (1tbsp) per 454g (1lb) soap. The oil is an antioxidant and particularly gentle. Good for facial soaps but label carefully as some people suffer from wheat allergies.

Saponification chart

It is absolutely essential that you use exactly the right amount of sodium hydroxide (caustic soda) to saponify your oils, that is, to turn them into soap. This is one area of soapmaking that calls for absolute precision since if an excess of sodium hydroxide remains in your soap, it can irritate or burn your skin. If you do not use enough sodium hydroxide, your soap will contain an unacceptable level of excess fat, which will result in a soft bar that could turn rancid.

The following chart was compiled by American soapmaker Elaine White and it gives you the saponification value of a number of oils. To use this chart, simply multiply the number of grams of oil by the figure stated and this will provide you with the exact amount of sodium hydroxide (caustic soda) required to saponify it. For example, 150 grams of olive oil requires 150 x 0.134 (the saponification value of olive oil), which equals 20.1 grams. If you are working in ounces, simply follow the the same procedure, remembering the amount of sodium hydroxide needed will be expressed in ounces.

NB: Most vegetable fats available in the U.K. supermarkets contain a high proportion of soya oil, so use 0.135 as the saponification value.

Several soapmakers have produced spreadsheets that will calculate the amount of sodium hydroxide for you. See internet resources (p79) for their email addresses.

- 0.135 apricot kernel oil, *Prunus armeniaca* oil
- 0.136 arachis oil, peanut oil, earthnut oil, katchung oil
- 0.133 avocado oil, *Persea americana* oil
- 0.175 babassu, Brazil nut oil
- 0.069 bayberry or myrtle wax
- 0.140 beef tallow, beef fat, beef suet, dripping
- 0.069 beeswax
- 0.136 borage oil, *Borago officinalis* oil
- 0.175 Brazil nut oil, babassu oil
- 0.124 canola oil, rapeseed oil, colza oil, rape oil, ramic oil
- 0.069 carnauba wax
- 0.128 castor oil, ricinus oil
- 0.138 chicken fat
- 0.137 cocoa butter
- 0.190 coconut oil, *Cocos nucifera* oil
- 0.132 cod liver oil
- 0.136 corn oil, maize oil
- 0.138 cottonseed oil
- 0.139 deer tallow, venison fat
- 0.136 evening primrose oil, *Oenothera biennis* oil
- 0.135 flax seed oil
- 0.139 goat tallow, goat fat

- 0.136 goose fat
- 0.123 to .135 grape seed oil, grapefruit seed oil, *Vitis vinifera* oil (varies widely)
- 0.136 hazelnut oil, *Corylus avellana* oil
- 0.1375 hemp oil, hemp seed oil
- 0.136 herring oil, fish oil
- 0.137 java cotton, kapok oil
- 0.069 jojoba oil
- 0.128 Karite butter, shea butter
- 0.135 kukui oil
- 0.074 lanolin, sheep wool fat
- 0.138 lard, pork tallow, pork fat
- 0.136 linseed oil, flax seed oil
- 0.139 macadamia nut oil, *Macadamia integrifolia* oil
- 0.136 margarine
- 0.140 mink oil
- 0.123 mustard seed oil
- 0.138 mutton tallow, sheep tallow
- 0.141 neat's foot oil, beef hoof oil
- 0.134 olive oil, loccu oil, Florence oil, *olium olivate*
- 0.141 palm oil
- 0.156 palm-kernel oil, palm butter
- 0.136 peanut oil, earthnut oil
- 0.135 pistachio oil
- 0.138 poppy-seed oil

- 0.135 pumpkin seed oil
- 0.128 rice bran oil
- 0.136 safflower oil
- 0.135 sardine oil, Japan fish oil
- 0.133 sesame seed oil, gigely oil
- 0.128 shea butter, African karite butter
- 0.138 sheep fat, sheep tallow
- 0.074 sheep wool fat, lanolin
- 0.136 shortening, vegetable shortening, hydrogenated vegetable oil
- 0.135 soybean oil, Chinese bean oil, *Hellanthus annuus* oil
- 0.134 sunflower seed oil
- 0.137 *Theobroma* oil, cocoa butter
- 0.137 tung oil, soybean oil, China wood oil, nut oil
- 0.138 venison fat, deer fat, deer or venison tallow
- 0.136 walnut oil, *Jugulans regia* oil
- 0.092 whale: sperm whale, body, blubber oil
- 0.102 whale: sperm whale, head
- 0.138 whale: baleen whale
- 0.132 wheatgerm oil, *Triticum vulgare* oil
- 0.074 wool fat, lanolin

Making scents

The choice of scent should be based on a number of elements. Firstly, the purpose of the soap. Is it designed for sensual languishing, cleaning and deodorizing or healing a sensitive skin? Do you want a fresh, crisp scent or a musky spicy fragrance? The second thing to consider is the stability of the essential oil. Some stand up better to the saponification process than others and several, particularly those within the citrus group, require a fixative such as benzoin or tea tree.

What are essential oils?

Essential oils are plant extracts usually obtained by distillation. Large amounts of plant matter are required to produce minute amounts of oil and this accounts for their relatively high cost.

Essential oil is powerful stuff and should be treated with respect. Always mix essential oils with a base oil such as almond before applying directly to the skin and wear rubber gloves when handling.

Do not use essential oils if you suffer from skin allergies or if you are in the first four months of pregnancy.

There is always a temptation to overload a soap with essential oils to increase the fragrance. Don't do it. As I have said, essential oils are powerful and using too much could cause skin irritation. If neat oil is accidentally splashed or rubbed in the eyes, flush the eyes with milk or clean warm water.

The healing properties of oils

Aromatherapists will tell you of the healing properties of many essential oils. Whilst it is debatable whether or not the saponification process kills these qualities, it is certainly true that fragrances can create and alter a mood and my tendency would be to select an essential oil on the assumption that its healing properties will be retained in the finished bar.

Fragrant alternatives

Synthetic fragrance oils, often cunningly packaged to resemble essentials, are a cheaper option. You can differentiate between them in two ways – by the price and the warning notice in small print that tells you not to use the oils on the skin. Whilst this warning should certainly be heeded if you intend to market your soap, the minute quantities required in soap make fragrance oils quite safe to use for this purpose. However, it is preferable not to use them for a particularly sensitive skin.

Making your own fragrances

Many soapmakers are tempted to create their own essential oils. In reality, however, the distillation process requires such large amounts of petals that the return is hardly worth it.

A useful and simple alternative for the home soapmaker is to infuse a base oil with fresh flowers and herbs before adding it to your soap. To do this, crush your petals or herbs to release the scent and pack them loosely in a wide necked bottle. Fill the bottle with olive, sunflower or almond oil and stir well. Cover the bottle opening with muslin, and place it in a sunny position (or a warm place), and leave for two weeks, shaking the bottle every day. Strain off the oil and refill the bottle with fresh plants. Repeat until the oil smells strongly of flowers or herbs. A similar process can be used with solid fats. Take coconut or vegetable fat and melt this in a saucepan filled with fresh petals or herbs. Stir continuously while the mixture cools. Re-melt the oil and drain off the petals, replacing these with a fresh batch. Repeat until the cooled fat smells strongly of the flowers or herbs.

It is also possible to infuse the water content of your soap in a similar way. Pour boiling water over a saucepan full of bruised petals or herbs and seal with a lid. Leave the flowers to infuse for two hours, then strain off the petals. Repeat until the water is strongly scented. By following this process you are creating a 'tea' or infusion. You can, of course, use commercial herbal teabags to achieve a similar result.

Possible problems

Both essential and fragrance oils can cause your soap to seize and, for this reason, it is wise to include them directly after trace when the sodium hydroxide (lye) is at its weakest. Should your soap begin to seize, whisk it rapidly with a stainless steel whisk and then pour immediately into the mould. They may also affect the colours you will achieve.

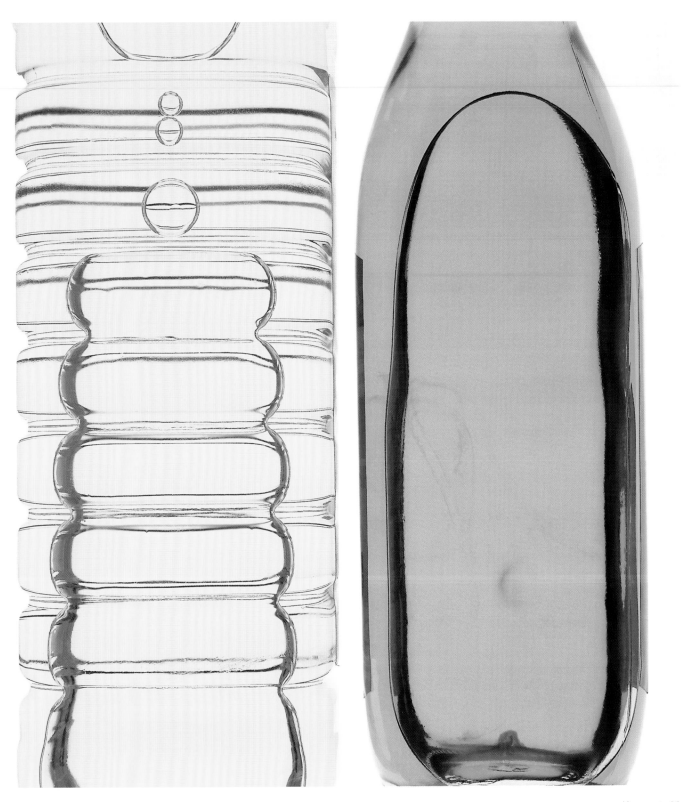

Mixing scents

Whilst many single essential oils will provide you with a delightful and recognizable fragrance, it is a gratifying experience to combine different oils and create your own personal perfumed masterpiece.

Before doing this, it is important to understand the principal of the 'three notes'. Notes are the categories used to define the strength and substance of a specific scent.

Oils in the 'top notes' category are the first to reach your nose, but can be fleeting. 'Middle notes' provide a solid centre to the fragrance. 'Base notes' act as a fixative and are perhaps the most sensual of the combination. As a rule of thumb, oils with a middle note should make up around 70 per cent of the total mix.

Below is a list of some of the most popular essential oils, together with their qualities. There are many essential oils that I have not had room to include, so do check out the bibliography (see p79) for further reading on this fascinating subject.

Bay *(Pimenta racemosa)*
BASE NOTE. Widely used in perfumery, this rich, aromatic oil is particularly sensual when mixed with nutmeg and mandarin. Makes for a great masculine soap.

Bergamot *(Citrus bergamia)*
TOP NOTE. Produced from orange rind. Bergamot is a clean, fresh, revitalizing scent often used in aftershaves. Good for greasy skin and recommended by aromatherapists for the treatment of eczema and acne.

Camomile, Roman *(Athemis nobilis)*
TOP NOTE. Distilled from the flowers and leaves of this common herb. Camomile is good for dry and sensitive skins and is recommended by aromatherapists to relieve acne and dermatitis. Great for facial soaps and steam baths. Clean, fresh scent.

Cardamom *(Elletaria cardamomum)*
TOP NOTE. Exotic spicy scent extracted from a plant seed. Relieves headaches and nausea.

Carrot *(Daucus carota)*
MIDDLE NOTE. Revitalizing scent, particularly good for sensitive skins and recommended by aromatherapists for the treatment of eczema and psoriasis.

Cedarwood *(Cedrus atlantica)*
BASE NOTE. Extracted from the wood of the cedar tree. Cedarwood provides a soft woody undertone that calms anxiety, especially when blended with sandalwood. Good antiseptic properties.

Citronella *(Cymbopogon nardus)*
TOP NOTE. Refreshing citrus fragrance. Extremely useful as a bug repellent and deodorant. Include citronella in dog shampoo bars to reduce the possibility of fleas.

Clary Sage *(Salvia sclarea)*
MIDDLE NOTE. Extracted from the flowers of the herb, clary sage is the scent to use if you love the smell of a country morning. This precious oil has antiseptic and deodorizing qualities.

Eucalyptus *(Eucalyptus globulus)*
TOP NOTE. Powerful, antiseptic scent. Useful as an insect and flea repellent. It is recommended by aromatherapists for relief from acne. It has anti-fungal properties and is a good ingredient to include in hand soaps.

Frankincense *(Boswellia carterii)*
BASE NOTE. Exotic, spicy, balsamic fragrance with antiseptic and revitalizing qualities. Good for ageing, oily or cracked skin. Use in a facial steam bath or lotion.

Geranium *(Pelargonium roseum)*
MIDDLE NOTE. Sweet, heady fragrance that benefits from combining with the sharper citrus or lavender oils. Anti-depressant qualities. Good for all skin types and recommended by aromatherapists for relief from eczema and dermatitis. Good ingredient for skin lotions.

Ginger *(Zingiber officinale)*
MIDDLE NOTE. Warm spicy fragrance with antiseptic qualities. Good addition to masculine soaps.

Grapefruit *(Citrus paradisi)* See lemon.

Howood Leaf *(Cinnamomum camphora)* See rosewood.

Lavender *(Lavendula officinalis)*
TOP NOTE. Fresh pungent fragrance with antiseptic and antibiotic qualities. Recommended for greasy and sensitive skin types. Also useful as an insect repellent.

Lemon (Citrus limonum)
TOP NOTE. Clear, strong fragrance that needs stabilizing in soap with a fixative such as benzoin. Good for greasy skins with anti-fungal and astringent qualities. Use together with a rough filler to exfoliate the skin.

Mandarin (Citrus reticulata) See tangerine.

Marjoram (Origanum marjorana)
TOP NOTE. Extracted from the flowers of the herb, marjoram has a warm leafy scent that blends well with lavender and citrus oils. Good for greasy skin due to its antiseptic qualities. Add to a footbath.

Myrrh (Commiphora myrrha)
BASE NOTE. Warm and woody. Good for the fingernails.

Neroli (Melaleuca viridiflora)
MIDDLE NOTE. Distilled from the blossom of the bitter orange tree, this pungent, sweet scent forms the basis of Eau de Cologne. It has revitalizing properties and is recommended by aromatherapists for the relief of dermatitis.

Patchouli (Pogostemon patchouli)
BASE NOTE. Love it or loathe it, patchouli is the oil of the swinging 1960s when it saturated the incense sticks of every self-respecting hippy. A warm peppery fragrance, patchouli has good antiseptic properties and is recommended for the relief of acne and eczema. It also deters dandruff, so consider using it in your shampoo bars.

Peppermint (Mentha piperata)
TOP NOTE. Clean, fresh and a little overpowering, peppermint essential oil is best used alone. With its antiseptic and insect repellent qualities, stimulating peppermint soap is a good choice for the morning-after-the-night-before. Peppermint should not be used during the first three months of pregnancy.

Pine (Pinus sylvestris)
MIDDLE NOTE. A classic soaper's scent, the fresh smell of pine helps the circulation and keeps the flies away. Ideal fragrance for men.

Rose otto (Rosa damascena)
MIDDLE NOTE. This very precious oil is wasted in soap. Whilst the heady scent of rose essential oil is seductive and its antiseptic qualities useful, shock at its cost could eliminate the anti-stress/depressant qualities it is said to contain. Try a rose fragrance oil instead.

Rosewood (Aniba parviflora)
MIDDLE NOTE. This sweet, spicy scent is distilled from a hardwood tree and its use is therefore environmentally unfriendly. Rosewood stimulates the skin cells and tissues and is beneficial to ageing skins. It is also an aphrodisiac, which probably explains why I have been politically incorrect and included it here. Howood leaf is said to be a good environmentally friendly alternative.

Sandalwood (Santalum album)
BASE NOTE. Warm, woody fragrance with antiseptic and astringent qualities. Sandalwood is good for dry and ageing skin and is recommended by aromatherapists for relief from eczema and skin irritations.

Tangerine/Mandarin (Citrus reticulata)
MIDDLE NOTE. Sweet tangy scent with antiseptic and soothing qualities. It is a good choice for facial oils and lotions. When using in soap, stabilize the scent with benzoin.

Tea tree (Melaleuca alternifolia)
TOP NOTE. A useful oil with a medicinal scent. Tea tree will act as a preservative in soap. Strong antiseptic and cleansing qualities and helpful for itchy skin, insect bites and acne.

Vanilla
BASE NOTE. Warm and welcoming oil with little else to recommend it except for its ability to make you constantly want to sniff (or lick) your bar of soap. Its inclusion also turns your soap dark brown.

Ylang ylang (Cananga odorata)
MIDDLE NOTE. A sweet heady scent that is beautiful on its own and also blends well with clary sage. Good for most skin types and particularly useful in shampoo bars and hair rinses as it acts as a tonic and promotes growth.

Colouring

Mixing and playing with colours is one of the many delights of soapmaking. Although your uncoloured soaps will harden into a wonderful range of creamy colours, you can enhance the natural look by adding liquefied herbs, vegetables and teas. You can also use powdered herbs and spices to create subtle colours.

Nevertheless, however hard you try, you will find colours very difficult to control as pigments react with fragrances and the caustic solution. They are also influenced by the natural colouring of your base oils. However, this does not apply when you are making soaps with a glycerine base. As saponification has already taken place, the caustic solution will not affect the colours and you can successfully use the normal liquid food colourings from your local supermarket.

Listed here are some ingredients that you probably already have in your kitchen.

Annato seeds – yellow
Caramelized sugar – brown
Carrot powder – orange
Cayenne – salmon
Cinnamon – beige
Cocoa – coffee to deep brown
Coffee – tan
Curry powder – yellowy-peach
Liquid chlorophyll – light green (tends to fade)
Paprika – peach
Plain cooking chocolate – brown
Spinach powder – pale green (speckles)
Turmeric – golden yellow

When using natural spices it is a good idea to mix them into a paste with a small quantity of soap from your soap pot and then stir the mixture back into the main base. This method will reduce the speckling caused by unmixed granules of spice.

The quantity that you use is a matter of personal taste but my advice is to start with tiny amounts and then build up. Try 5ml (1tsp) per 454g (1lb) of oil. Too much colour will stain your hands, the bath and your towels. You want to aim for a white lather no matter how deep the colour of your soap.

The lapis blues and brilliant greens that occur in mass produced soaps are achieved by using natural ultramarines and oxides or specific pigment powders created for cosmetic use. Stockists for these are included on p79. You can buy other cosmetic pigments from specialist suppliers. Always check that they are certified for use with cosmetics.

You can successfully mix natural ultramarines and oxides with manmade pigments but the colours you end up with will be a matter of trial and error. Blue pigment, depending on the type of base oil in your soap, can produce pink soap. This is fine if you want pink soap, but very frustrating if you were hoping for blue. The inclusion of honey-coloured beeswax and milk of any kind produces a tan coloured soap base. If you add blue pigment to this, the result will be a green soap. Some flavourings also turn soap brown – the most common of these being vanilla extract. Goat's milk also tends to turn soap a pale

tan colour. Colourings are best added at trace after the addition of essential oils as these can also affect the basic colour of your soap.

Bright colours also have an irritating tendency to fade. Make a test batch and store half in a dark place and the rest in bright light. Check the variation after several weeks to test for colour stability.

Oxides and cosmetic pigments

When using an ultramarine or an oxide in a 1kg (2lb) batch of soap, dissolve approximately 4ml ($^3/_4$tsp) of dry powder in 28.25g (1oz) of warm distilled water. Reduce the water content of your soap recipe by 28.25g (1oz) to counteract this. Add the diluted colourant to the soap mix with a dropper so you can control the colour density. Bear in mind that your soap will look considerably darker in the pot than after it has set. When using cosmetic pigments, less powder is required. Dissolve only .30cc (cover the tip of a teaspoon) of pigment in 28.25g (1oz) of water, then proceed as above.

Experiment with ultramarines, which are available in various colours and also ochres and iron oxides. Take great care not to ingest pigments as they do have varying levels of toxicity.

Lori Schenkelberg, a very enterprising person in the US, now packages very small quantities of oxides and cosmetic pigments. She sells her pigment packs by mail order together with a very useful information sheet (see p79).

Wax chips

These are designed for candlemaking and can be used with some success in soap. However, if you intend to sell your soap in Europe, be warned that it will not meet cosmetics legislation requirements. This will also apply to soap made with wax crayons, which some soapmakers like to melt down and use as colourants.

Colours can be mixed and matched to create your own shades. Dissolve slivers from the chips in soap mix taken from the pot and then return to the batch, stirring until evenly mixed.

Soap colourings

Various UK craft manufacturers sell liquid as 'soap colouring'. This is designed for use with melt and pour glycerine soap but unfortunately seldom survives the sodium hydroxide (lye) during the saponification process.

Above: Various shades of colours have been achieved using a base made from coconut, palm and vegetable oils.

Meltdown

Re-batching is the term used for reconstituting cured and part cured cold-processed soaps. This technique offers several major advantages. Firstly, it greatly reduces the possibility of the sodium hydroxide (lye) in your soap distorting colourings and fragrances. Secondly, it allows you to recycle trimmings and misshapen soaps, thereby totally eliminating any wastage.

Brighter colours can be achieved and fragrances will last longer when added to a re-batch and you can also add fresh herbs and flower petals and reduce the risk of discolouration. Re-batched soaps can be poured into fancy moulds as you are no longer limited to using plastic, glass or stainless steel.

Re-batching step-by-step

Step 1: Make your basic soap in the normal way and set it aside until it is good and hard (at least one month).

Step 2: Use a cheese grater, an electric food processor or an old fashioned mincer to grind the soap to a fine consistency.

Step 3: Weigh the ground soap and set aside 339g (12oz) of warm distilled or spring water per 454g (1lb) soap.

Step 4: Put the ground soap and three quarters of the water in a double boiler (or in a bowl placed in a saucepan half full of water), over a medium heat and stir until all the soap is wet. Add the remaining water and stir again.

Step 5: Cover the pot and leave to simmer. The melting down process could take up to an hour and the soap should be stirred intermittently until all the lumps have dissolved.

Step 6: When the soap has reached a smooth creamy consistency, remove it from the heat and add your colouring, fragrance and/or fillers. Stir until they are evenly distributed. The consistency of the soap mix may change when you add the fragrance oils. If it thins, keep stirring until smooth and creamy. If it thickens, add more water and stir rapidly.

Step 7: Continue to stir until the mixture cools. Pour it into pre-greased moulds and leave to set in the normal way. If you are unhappy with the results of a soap made from a melt and pour, simply re-melt it in a double boiler over a low heat.

Recycling soap

When recycling soap leftovers, follow the same procedure as above. Your leftovers may contain many different colours and textures and for this reason you will never create a pure white soap or a flat creamy bar. Use your recycled batches for herbal or oatmeal soaps where texture becomes a feature. Try substituting the water for goat's milk or a mix of half water, half goat's milk to create a nice rich soap. You can also create soaps with layers of colours by melting down small amounts of soap and adding different colourings to each batch. When working with melt and pour soaps, wipe the surface of each layer with witch hazel. This will help one layer adhere to another.

Using offcuts and failed batches

With a little creative thought you will find many uses for your soap scraps and failed batches. Whilst a failed soap may be too caustic to use on your skin, it could still serve as a fragrant room or drawer scenter. You could also cut the soap into small cubes and string them together. Hang them as light pulls or use as key fobs. Strings of soap can be hung from clothes hangers to freshen and fragrance clothes. Put a fragranced bar in your laundry or underwear drawer and everything will come out smelling fresh.

Many soaps are insect repellents. Chunks of suitably fragranced soap will help to keep moths away.

Leftover scraps of good soap can be grated and put in a muslin bag with 15ml (1tbsp) of oatmeal. Use as an exfoliating scrub.

You can incorporate offcuts of good soap with melt and pour soap base. Arrange them in the mould and pour the melted soap base over the top.

Basic instructions

The following instructions show you how to make real soap (by saponifying the oils from scratch) and how to work with a ready-made soap base. The first method most certainly produces a richer, creamier bar of soap but the second lets you use colour and fragrance freely and eliminates the need to use sodium hydroxide. Whichever method you choose, follow the instructions carefully and you will end up with bubbles to be proud of.

The cold-process method

Although many different ingredients can be used in cold-process soapmaking, the basic cold-process method always remains the same. Simply follow the instructions below:

Step 1: Weigh out your base fats, oils, beeswax and butters (if required) on accurate weighing scales and put them into a stainless steel or enamel pan.

Step 2: Place the pan over a low heat until the contents have melted. Turn off the heat and leave until oils reach approximately 49°C (120°F). Stir intermittently.

Step 3: Put on protective glasses and rubber gloves, then carefully weigh out your sodium hydroxide (lye) and place it in a plastic or glass container. Make sure you do this outside or in a well-ventilated room.

Step 4: Now weigh the water on the scales and pour it into another plastic or glass jug or bucket. Pour the sodium hydroxide (lye) granules into the water and stir until dissolved. The reaction of sodium hydroxide (lye) to water produces heat. Leave until temperature settles at around 49°C (120°F). Take care not to breathe in the fumes. Pour the lye/water into the fats, and stir with a stainless steel or plastic spoon or spatula.

Step 5: Continue to stir occasionally until the mixture reaches the stage when soap dribbled from the spatula will leave a faint trace line on the surface. This stage is known as 'light trace'. If you require a heavy trace, leave the mixture to thicken, but you should still be able to pour it.

Step 6: Add scent and stir thoroughly. Then add the colouring and stir well. Add herbs, fillers and essential oils as required.

Step 7: Stir and then pour into a greased mould. Leave to set for 24 hours or until hard. Turn the soap out of the mould and cut into bars.

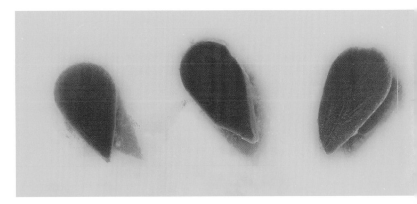

Using a ready-made soap base

For those of you who are nervous of using caustic solutions, the use of ready-made glycerine soap bases can be great fun and will still allow you to exercise your creativity.

Melt and pour is the perfect solution for the impatient (or children), and there are a number of recipes in this book that will teach you how to make scrumptious soaps using this simple method.

Both clear and opaque melt and pour soap bases are available, although most of them do contain a high level of artificial ingredients. It is possible to buy a pure vegetable glycerine base but by nature this is usually a pale yellow colour and you need to take this into account when designing your soap.

Simply follow these instructions to make an array of delightful soaps:

Step 1: Cut the soap base into small chunks and place them in either a double saucepan or a bowl standing in a saucepan half-full of water. Put the saucepan on a very low heat and cover the top of the pan with cling film.

Step 2: Once the soap has melted, add colour and fragrance and pour the mixture into a mould. Leave to set hard – this should take about ten minutes.

Soap en-croûte

There are all manner of interesting ways that you can wrap your soap and I hope you can take a few of my ideas and make them your own.

Handmade papers look wonderful with natural soaps and, if you don't want to make your own, you will find plenty available to complement your ingredients. For example, you can buy papers made with coconut and banana fibres as well as some with petals embedded in them. For some great papermaking ideas, check out Angela Ramsay's *The Handmade Paper Book*. Take note, however, that glycerine melt and pour soaps tend to sweat and should always be wrapped in plastic film before you use an outer wrap of paper.

You can also use leaves and twigs to add finishing touches to your soaps. Make little parcels or bands with banana and palm leaves and secure them with natural raffia. Don't be tempted to use coloured raffias though as the dye will bleed onto your soap. A decorative twig tied into the knot makes a pretty finishing touch.

If you like the idea of wrapping your soap into a little parcel you might like to cut a shape out of the middle so that admirers can see and smell the delicious contents.

Opposite: Papers, fabrics, ribbons and boxes in earthy colours enhance the natural feel of handmade soaps.

Above: Brightly coloured tissue paper, plastic wrap and ribbons are striking. This type of wrapping is fun and is great for a birthday or Christmas gift.

Left: Sophisticated white and silver packaging is extremely elegant. Wrapped in this way, handmade soaps are an extra special gift.

RECIPES

Cocktails

The clearness of a glycerine soap base always reminds me of ice; add colour, flavour and bubbles and you can produce all manner of exotic soap cocktails on which to feast your skin. Remember that these cocktails should be stirred rather than shaken.

Tequila sunrise

Wonderful rainbow effects can be achieved by allowing colours to blend into one another. This, of course, might occur naturally if you make your soap after happy hour rather than before!

Soap style
Lovely sun-shaped jellies. No particular beneficial properties, but very pretty in the bathroom.

Ingredients
1kg (2lb) clear glycerine soap base
5ml (1tsp) fragrance or essential oil of your choice
Red, orange and yellow liquid food colouring

Equipment
Sharp knife
3 plastic or glass jugs
3 stainless steel or enamel saucepans
Sun mould (by Milky Way Moulds)

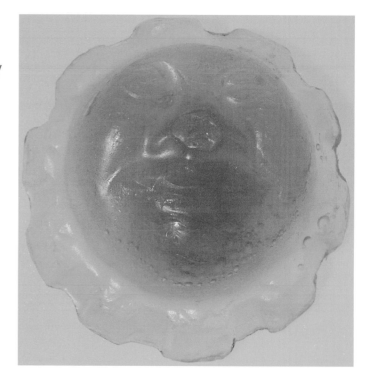

Method
Cut the soap base into rough chunks and place in one of the jugs. Stand all three jugs (two of which are empty for the moment) in saucepans half-full of water. Heat the water until the soap begins to melt in the jug. Keeping the heat as low as possible, cover the saucepan that contains the soap. When the soap has completely melted, add the fragrance or essential oil.

Then divide the soap equally between the three saucepans. Add a different colour to each batch and stir gently.

Pour the red soap into the bottom of each mould then pour the orange soap directly on top followed by the yellow soap. Leave to set. When hard, turn the mould over and push out the soap. Trim off any rough edges with a sharp knife. Serve with a smile.

Crème de menthe

Use miniature cookie cutters to cut interesting shapes from leftover soaps, or make curls by running a potato peeler over the surface. Arrange these in a mould and then pour over a glycerine soap base. Here I have used a leaf shaped cutter to resemble mint leaves, albeit red ones.

Soap Style
Invigorating – a great foot deodorizer.

Ingredients
1kg (2lb) clear glycerine soap base
Leftover scraps cold-processed soap
5ml (1tsp) mint fragrance or essential oil
Green liquid food colouring

Equipment
Sharp knife
Plastic or glass jug
Stainless steel or enamel saucepan
Cookie cutters
Mould of your choice

Method
Cut the soap base into rough chunks and place them in a plastic or glass jug. Stand the jug in a saucepan half-full of water and place on the stove over a low heat. Keeping the heat as low as possible, let the soap melt in the jug. Cover the saucepan.

Whilst waiting for the soap to melt, cut some leaf shapes out of leftover soap and arrange in the mould. When the soap has completely melted, add the fragrance or essential oil and just a couple of drops of colouring. Pour the soap in the mould over the leaf shapes.

Leave to set. When hard, turn the mould over and push out the soap. Trim off any rough edges with a sharp knife.

Pina colada

For this recipe I have topped a pure coconut cold-processed soap with a layer of glycerine base scented with pineapple fragrance. If you don't want to go to the trouble of making a cold processed soap, the same visual effect can be achieved using an opaque melt and pour base.

Soap style
Creamy with big bubbles. A lovely holiday soap.

Ingredients (for the base)
850g (30oz) coconut oil
57g (2oz) cocoa butter
168g (6oz) sodium hydroxide (lye)
340g (12oz) water
5ml (1tsp) coconut fragrance

(for the top)
112g (4oz) clear glycerine soap base
3 drops pineapple fragrance
Yellow liquid food colouring
Witch hazel

Equipment
Stainless steel or enamel saucepan
Protective glasses
Rubber gloves
Wooden, plastic or stainless steel spoon
2 glass thermometers
Square plastic tray
Sharp knife
Plastic or glass jug

Method
To make the base:
Place the coconut oil and cocoa butter into a stainless steel or enamel saucepan and heat until melted. Wearing eye protection and rubber gloves, add the sodium hydroxide (lye) to the water and stir.

Place a glass thermometer into the oils and the lye solution and when their temperatures both reach 49°C (120°F) pour the lye into the oils and stir with a wooden, plastic or stainless steel spoon.

Grease a square plastic tray (or line a cardboard box with a dustbin bag) to use as a mould.

When the soap reaches trace (see Basic instructions, p27), add the fragrance oil and stir. Pour the soap into the mould and leave until firm (several hours or overnight).

To make the top:
Cut the clear soap base into rough chunks and place in a plastic or glass jug.

Stand the jug in a saucepan half-full of water and place this on the stove. Heat the water until the soap begins to melt in the jug. Keeping the heat as low as possible, cover the saucepan. When the soap has completely melted, add the pineapple fragrance and the colouring. Stir gently to avoid air bubbles.

Wipe over or spray the surface of the coconut soap base with witch hazel. Pour the glycerine soap on top of the base. Gently shake the mould so that the topping is evenly distributed. Leave to set.

Turn out of the mould and cut into chunks. Leave to cure in a well ventilated place for four weeks before use.

Bucks fizz

This delicious orange scented soap should be used together with a Bath fizzer (see p72). Let the bath ball fizz in your tub, then lather yourself with a rich combination of creamy soap and mango butter.

Soap style
Rich and creamy with slow bubbles.

Ingredients
340g (12oz) coconut oil
283.5g (10oz) palm oil
226g (8oz) olive oil
58g (2oz) apricot kernel oil
58g (2oz) mango butter
131g (4$^{1}/_{2}$oz) sodium hydroxide (lye)
340g (12oz) water
2.5ml ($^{1}/_{2}$ tsp) diluted D&C orange 5
  pigment powder
2.5ml ($^{1}/_{2}$ tsp) sweet orange essential oil
2.5ml ($^{1}/_{2}$ tsp) May Chang essential oil

Equipment
Stainless steel or enamel saucepan
Protective glasses
Rubber gloves
Wooden, plastic or stainless steel spoon
2 glass thermometers
Plastic tray or mould of your choice
Blanket
Sharp knife or cheesewire

Method
Place the base oils and mango butter into a stainless steel or enamel saucepan and heat until melted.

Wearing eye protection and rubber gloves, add the sodium hydroxide (lye) to the water and stir.

Place a glass thermometer into the oils and the lye solution and when their temperatures both reach 49°C (120°F) pour the lye into the oils and stir with a wooden, plastic or stainless steel spoon. Grease your mould.

When the soap reaches trace (see Basic instructions, p27), add the colouring and stir until it is evenly distributed. Blend the essential oils together and add to the soap. Cover the soap with a blanket and leave for 48 hours or until hard.

Turn out of mould and cut into blocks with a sharp knife or cheesewire. Leave to cure for four weeks before use

Vodka on the rocks

One of the main advantages of using a clear glycerine soap base is that you can place all sorts of fun things inside the soap. In this recipe I have poured the soap over some leftover chunks of cold-processed soaps and some small plastic pink elephants that I found in a bead shop. They seemed quite appropriate for the cocktail section!

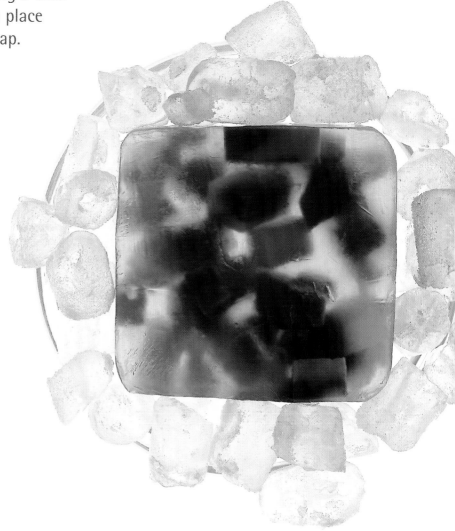

Soap style
Simple to make and a great party piece.

Ingredients
Leftover scraps of cold-processed soap
 or half a bar of shop-bought soap
1kg (2lb) clear glycerine soap base
5ml (1tsp) fragrance or essential oil of your
 choice

Equipment
Sharp knife
Plastic or glass jug
Stainless steel or enamel saucepan
Plastic spatula
Square plastic container or mould of your choice
Small plastic elephants
Wooden chopstick or kebab skewer

Method
Cut the cold-processed soap into 1cm ($1/2$in) cubes. Cut the soap base into rough chunks and place them in a plastic or glass jug.

Stand the jug in a saucepan half-full of water and place on the stove.

Heat the water until the soap begins to melt in the jug. Keeping the heat as low as possible, cover the saucepan. When the soap has completely melted, add the fragrance or essential oil. Stir gently to avoid air bubbles.

Pour the melted soap into the mould. While the soap is still liquid, add the cold processed soap cubes and the plastic elephants, a few at a time. Gently push the elephants under the surface with the wooden chopstick or skewer so that they are positioned throughout the soap rather than just on the surface. Leave to set.

Turn the soap out of the mould. Finally, cut into bars, taking care not to cut through a plastic elephant.

Appetizers

Many of the most appetizing plants and fruits are equally good for your skin and in these recipes I have tried to balance luscious colours and flavours with the very best skin food. You can make your soaps look even more appealing by cutting them in interesting ways and by adding dried plants, fruits, petals or seeds to the surface before the soap sets.

Melon slice

There are some wonderful melon fragrances on the market, and they make the perfect soap to use when you are feeling fruity. If you prefer canteloupe to watermelon, use orange colouring instead of red. Perfectionists can dry their own melon seeds instead of using any of a huge variety of decorative seeds available in Asian supermarkets.

Soap style
Big, bold and fruity.

Ingredients
1kg (2lb) clear glycerine
   soap base
5ml (1tsp) melon fragrance oil
Red liquid food colouring
Handful of dried black seeds

Equipment
Sharp knife
Plastic or glass jug
Stainless steel or enamel
   saucepan
Wooden, plastic or stainless
   steel spoon
Half-round mould
Wooden chopstick
   or kebab skewer

Method
Cut the soap base into rough chunks and place them in a plastic or glass jug. Stand the jug in a saucepan half-full of water and place this on the stove. Heat the water until the soap begins to melt in the jug. Keeping the heat as low as possible, cover the saucepan. When the soap has completely melted, add the fragrance, then add five or six drops of colouring. Stir this in gently to avoid air bubbles.

Pour the soap into the mould. While it is still semi-liquid, arrange the seeds in a strip along the centre of the surface of the soap and let them sink gently. (Note: if a skin has formed on the soap, push the seeds gently through using a chopstick or skewer).

Leave to set – you could place it in the fridge if you are in a hurry. When hard, turn the mould over and push out the soap. Cut it into half-moon-shaped slices and trim off any rough edges with a sharp knife.

Seaweed starter

Seaweed can be bought in an Asian supermarket or health food shop. Alternatively, you can find bladderwrack on the beach and hang it up to dry. Powdered kelp can be bought from herbal suppliers and produces a nice natural green colour. It does have a strong smell, but that disappears in time. Seaweed improves the texture and colour of the skin and can also add a very decorative, natural element to your soap.

Soap style
Very Feng Shui in all respects.

Ingredients
400g (14oz) coconut oil
400g (14oz) olive oil
200g (7oz) vegetable oil
58g (2oz) beeswax
153g (5$^{1}/_{2}$oz) sodium hydroxide (lye)
396g (14oz) water
5ml (1tsp) rosemary essential oil
5ml (1tsp) lavender essential oil
15ml (1tbsp) kelp
Sprigs of dried seaweed

Equipment
Stainless steel or enamel saucepan
Protective glasses
Rubber gloves
Wooden, plastic or stainless steel spoon
2 glass thermometers
Plastic tray or mould of your choice
Blanket
Sharp knife or cheesewire

Method
Place the base oils and beeswax into a stainless steel or enamel saucepan and heat until melted. Wearing eye protection and rubber gloves, add the sodium hydroxide (lye) to the water and stir.

Place a glass thermometer into the oils and the lye solution and when their temperatures both reach 49°C (120°F), pour the lye into the oils and stir with a wooden, plastic or stainless steel spoon. Grease your mould.

When the soap reaches trace (see Basic instructions, p27), add the essential oils (blended together) and the kelp and stir until evenly distributed. Pour into the mould and place dried seaweed on the surface of the soap. Cover the soap with a blanket and leave for 48 hours or until hard.

Turn out of the mould and cut the soap into bars with a sharp knife or cheesewire. Leave to cure in a well-ventilated place for four weeks before use.

Sushi

As all Japanese food lovers know, the very best sushi is made from raw ingredients. Therefore, in true tradition, I am not going to give you a definitive recipe for this soap, just a few ideas. All you need is a plastic tray, some interesting cutters and an addiction to soapmaking.

As you become a fully fledged soapmaker you will find that, when you have filled your mould, you are inevitably left with soap in your pot that you just cannot squeeze in. There isn't enough to justify a new mould but there is too much to waste and, besides, you need to get rid of it so that you can clean your soap pot.

The answer is to keep a plastic tray close at hand and to build up layers of soap as and when you make a new batch. The result is a highly interesting multi-coloured and scented soap bar that can be cut into some interesting shapes and sizes for guest soaps.

To cut the soap, use cookie cutters, a serrated chopper or simply a sharp knife. You can decorate the surface of the soaps with seaweed, which can be stuck on with a little bit of melted soap. You can also wrap the soaps in leaves and tie them with raffia. Packaged in a bamboo basket, your leftovers will be transformed into an excellent gift for your favourite minimalist.

The best sushi soaps combine leftover seaweed soap, Bucks Fizz and natural creamy white soap. A touch of black (created with black oxide pigment) also adds to the overall effect. When pouring a fresh layer of cold-processed soap onto a set layer, score the bottom layer with a fork and wet it slightly to make sure the layers do not separate. When using soap made with a glycerine base, wipe over each layer with witch hazel.

Seafood in aspic

This glycerine soap is full of fare gathered at my local beach. I dried the bladderwrack for several weeks until the pockets of moisture had disappeared. As an alternative you can use dried seaweed. The little shells were boiled thoroughly before use. For a mould, I have used a standard loaf tin that conveniently made a perfect 1kg (2lb) ingot of soap. If you want to take the idea a step further, why not add some plastic fish, or even a plastic prawn or two?

Soap style
Great dinner party centrepiece.

Ingredients
1kg (2lb) clear glycerine soap base
5ml (1tsp) rosewood essential oil
(or fragrance of your choice)
Green liquid food colouring
Handful of dried seaweed
Handful of cockle shells

Equipment
Sharp knife
Plastic or glass jug
Stainless steel or enamel saucepan
Wooden, plastic or stainless steel spoon
Mould of your choice
Toothpick

Method
Cut the soap base into rough chunks and place them in a plastic or glass jug. Stand the jug in a saucepan half-full of water and place on the stove. Heat the water until the soap begins to melt in the jug. Keeping the heat as low as possible, cover the saucepan. When the soap has completely melted, add the essential oil or fragrance, then add just two or three drops of colouring. Stir this in gently to avoid air bubbles.

Pour the soap into the mould. While it is still liquid, arrange the seaweed and shells on the surface of the soap and let them sink gently. (Note: if a skin has formed on the soap, push the shells and seaweed gently through using a toothpick.)

Leave to set – you could place it in the fridge if you are in a hurry. When hard, turn the mould over and push out the soap. Trim off any rough edges with a sharp knife.

After everyone has admired your masterpiece, cut into slices.

Avocado melt

This soap combines the moisturizing benefits of avocado oil with the firm texture provided by shea butter. I have used lemon tea tree oil as the scent, but it is quite costly. Melissa fragrance is a good alternative, or you can use plain lemon oil mixed with a little kaolin to help it hold up in the soap.

Soap style
Rich, creamy and moisturizing.

Ingredients
400g (14oz) coconut oil
400g (14oz) vegetable oil
200g (7oz) avocado oil
8g (2oz) shea butter
156g (5¹/₂oz) sodium hydroxide (lye)
378g (13oz) water
10ml (2tsp) lemon tea tree essential oil
2.5ml (¹/₂ tsp) May Chang essential oil
5ml (1tsp) green cosmetic clay

Equipment
Stainless steel or enamel saucepan
Protective glasses
Rubber gloves
Wooden, plastic or stainless steel spoon
2 glass thermometers
2 plastic or glass jugs
Plastic tray or mould of your choice
Wooden chopstick or kebab skewer
Blanket
Sharp knife or cheesewire

Method
Place the base oils and shea butter into a stainless steel or enamel saucepan and heat until melted. Wearing eye protection and rubber gloves, add the sodium hydroxide (lye) to the water and stir.

Place a glass thermometer into the oils and the lye solution and when their temperatures both reach 49°C (120°F) pour the lye into the oils and stir with a wooden, plastic or stainless steel spoon. Grease your mould.

When the soap reaches trace (see Basic instructions, p27), add the essential oils and stir. Then divide the batch into two jugs. Add the colouring to one half and stir until it is evenly distributed. Pour the two jugs of soap into the mould alternately so you have a mixture of the two colours throughout. Gently stir the soap with the chopstick or skewer to create a marbled effect. Cover the soap with a blanket and leave for 48 hours or until it is hard.

Turn out of mould and cut into blocks with a sharp knife or cheesewire. Leave to cure for four weeks before use.

Herb and nut pâtés

Texture is a very important part of soapmaking, and exciting effects can be achieved by adding dried herbs, seeds or powdered citrus rind. If you add these to the whole batch you will create an exfoliating scrub. Alternatively, split your batch into two and put your natural additives into just one half, pouring the soap in two layers. This gives you the advantage of a dual soap, textured on one side and silky smooth on the other.

Rosehip and ginger pâté

The warm scent of ginger blends perfectly with ylang ylang, wild rosehips and rosehip seed oil. A touch of cocoa butter will help to protect your skin from wrinkles.

Soap style
Superbly speckled with creamy and moisturizing bubbles.

Ingredients
400g (14oz) coconut oil
200g (7oz) vegetable oil
300g (10^1/$_2$oz) olive oil
100g (3^1/$_2$oz) rosehip seed oil
58g (2oz) cocoa butter
156g (5^1/$_2$oz) sodium hydroxide (lye)
396g (14oz) water
5ml (1tsp) vitamin E oil
5ml (1tsp) ginger essential oil
5ml (1tsp) ylang ylang essential oil
Handful of dried, ground rosehip shells

Equipment
Stainless steel or enamel saucepan
Protective glasses
Rubber gloves
Wooden, plastic or stainless steel spoon
2 glass thermometers
Plastic tray or mould of your choice
Blanket
Sharp knife or cheesewire

Method
Place the coconut, vegetable, olive and rosehip oils with the cocoa butter in a stainless steel or enamel saucepan and heat until melted. Wearing eye protection and rubber gloves, add the sodium hydroxide (lye) to the water and stir.

Place a glass thermometer into the oils and the lye solution and when their temperatures both reach 49°C (120°F), pour the lye into the oils and stir with a wooden, plastic or stainless steel spoon. Grease your mould.

When the soap reaches trace (see Basic instructions, p27), add the vitamin E oil and blend together the essential oils, add to the soap and stir. Sprinkle in the ground rosehips and stir until evenly distributed. Pour the soap into the mould.

Cover with a blanket and leave for 48 hours or until hard.

Turn out of the mould and cut into blocks with a sharp knife or cheesewire. Leave to cure for four weeks before use.

Dock, nettle and lemongrass pâté

This herby delight makes an invigorating and soothing bar of soap that is excellent for those with sensitive skin. Vitamin E and benzoin are added to preserve the fresh dock leaf mixture.

Soap style
Gentle but exfoliating. Good creamy, refreshing bubbles.

Ingredients
400g (14oz) coconut oil
300g (10^1/$_2$oz) palm oil
100g (3^1/$_2$oz) olive oil
200g (7oz) vegetable oil
28g (1oz) beeswax
3 medium-sized dock leaves
385g (13^1/$_2$oz) water
153g (5^1/$_2$oz) sodium hydroxide (lye)
5ml (1tsp) vitamin E oil
5ml (1tsp) benzoin
10g (^{1}/$_4$oz) dried nettles and dried lemongrass (mixed)
15ml (1tbsp) lemongrass essential oil

Equipment
Stainless steel or enamel saucepan
Liquidizer
Plastic or glass jug
Protective glasses
Rubber gloves
2 glass thermometers
Wooden, plastic or stainless steel spoon
Plastic tray or mould of your choice
Blanket
Sharp knife or cheesewire

Method
Place the coconut, palm, olive and vegetable oils and the beeswax into a stainless steel or enamel saucepan and heat until melted.

Place the dock leaves in a liquidizer with 150g (5^1/$_4$oz) of the water and liquidize to a fine pulp. Pour this mixture into the jug with the remaining water.

Wearing eye protection and rubber gloves, add the sodium hydroxide (lye) to the dock leaf solution and stir.

Place a glass thermometer into the oils and the lye solution and when their temperatures both reach 49°C (120°F), pour the lye into the oils and stir with a wooden, plastic or stainless steel spoon.

Grease your selected mould. When the soap reaches light trace (see Basic instructions, p27), add the vitamin E and benzoin. Then add the dried nettle and lemongrass mixture followed by the lemongrass essential oil. Stir until fully traced. Pour into the moulds.

Cover the soap with a blanket and leave for 48 hours or until hard. Turn out of the mould and cut into blocks with a sharp knife or cheesewire.

Leave to cure for four weeks. Serve just before breakfast!

Walnut and orange loaf

This is a real epicure's delight. Walnut is quite a heavy oil and, if you prefer, you can substitute it with apricot kernel oil. The inclusion of oatmeal depends on whether you want a textured or silky smooth bar. Either way, it's delicious.

Soap style
Rich and mildly astringent.

Ingredients
400g (14oz) coconut oil
400g (14oz) palm oil
100g (3¹/₂oz) olive oil
100g (3¹/₂oz) walnut oil
151g (5¹/₂oz) sodium hydroxide (lye)
375g (13oz) water
10ml (2tsp) vitamin E oil
15ml (1tbsp) bergamot essential oil
30ml (2tbsp) finely ground oatmeal
4 drops diluted orange cosmetic pigment

Equipment
Stainless steel or enamel saucepan
Protective glasses
Rubber gloves
2 glass thermometers
Wooden, plastic or stainless steel spoon
Plastic tray or mould of your choice
Wooden chopstick or kebab skewer
Blanket
Sharp knife or cheesewire

Method
Place the coconut, palm, olive and walnut oils in a stainless steel or enamel saucepan and heat until melted.

Wearing eye protection and rubber gloves, add the sodium hydroxide (lye) to the water and stir. Place a glass thermometer into the oils and the lye solution and when their temperatures both reach 49°C (120°F), pour the lye into the oils and stir with a wooden, plastic or stainless steel spoon.

Grease your selected mould. When the soap reaches light trace (see Basic instructions, p27), add the vitamin E and

essential oil and stir well. Divide the batch in two. Add the oatmeal to one half and the orange colourant to the other. Stir both pots well.

Pour the two soaps alternately into the mould and swirl with a chopstick or skewer.

Cover the soap with a blanket and leave for 48 hours or until it is nearly hard.

Turn the soap out of the mould and cut into blocks with a sharp knife or cheesewire.

Leave to cure for four weeks before use.

Creamy lavender

Nothing clears the senses like the fresh aroma of lavender. Here it is blended with rich cocoa butter, with just a splash of evening primrose oil, swirled into a summer delicacy.

Soap style

Refreshing, relaxing and definitely dreamy. Oodles of creamy bubbles.

Ingredients

350g (12¹/₄oz) coconut oil
250g (8³/₄oz) palm oil
350g (12¹/₄oz) vegetable oil
28g (1oz) cocoa butter
151g (5¹/₂oz) sodium hydroxide (lye)
367g (13oz) water
50g (1³/₄oz) evening primrose oil
15ml (1tbsp) lavender essential oil
30ml (2tbsp) diluted mauve pigment
Dried lavender buds

Equipment

Stainless steel or enamel saucepan
Protective glasses
Rubber gloves
2 glass thermometers
Wooden, plastic or stainless steel spoon
Plastic tray or mould of your choice
Wooden chopstick or kebab skewer
Blanket
Sharp knife or cheesewire

Method

Place the coconut, palm and vegetable oils together with the cocoa butter in a stainless steel or enamel saucepan and heat until melted.

Wearing eye protection and rubber gloves, add the sodium hydroxide (lye) to the water and stir. Place a glass thermometer into the oils and the lye solution and when their temperatures both reach 49°C (120°F), pour the lye into the oils and stir with a wooden, plastic or stainless steel spoon.

Grease your selected mould. When the soap reaches light trace (see Basic instructions, p27), add the evening primrose and essential oil and divide the batch into two. Add the colour to one half. Pour alternately into the mould and swirl with the chopstick or skewer to create a marbled effect. Press lavender buds into the top of the soap while it is still gooey. Cover the soap with a blanket and leave for 48 hours or until hard.

Turn out of the mould and cut into blocks with a sharp knife or cheesewire. Leave to cure for four weeks.

Salads

Since I turned veggie three years ago, I hope I haven't disappointed some readers by staying well away from tallow, lard and Emu oil. Fortunately, you can make wonderful skin care products with the fruit of the earth.

Olive, mango and jojoba

You can use this soap as a shampoo bar as it contains a rich combination of oils to condition your hair. It is equally good for your complexion. When using soap on your hair, it is a good idea to add 15ml (1tbsp) of either lemon juice or cider vinegar to your final rinse.

Soap style
Rich, creamy and fruity.

Ingredients
200g (7oz) palm oil
800g (27¹/₂oz) olive oil
28g (1oz) beeswax
15ml (1tbsp) mango butter
138g (5oz) sodium hydroxide (lye)
369g (12¹/₂oz) water
10ml (2tsp) mango fragrance
10ml (2tsp) jojoba oil
5ml (1tsp) diluted orange cosmetic
   pigment

Equipment
Stainless steel or enamel saucepan
Protective glasses
Rubber gloves
Wooden, plastic or stainless steel spoon
2 glass thermometers
Plastic tray or mould of your choice
Wooden chopstick or skewer
Sharp knife or cheesewire

Method
Place the palm and olive oils together with the beeswax and mango butter into a stainless steel or enamel saucepan and heat until melted.

Wearing eye protection and rubber gloves, add the sodium hydroxide (lye) to the water and stir. Place a glass thermometer into the oils and the lye solution and when their temperatures both reach 49°C (120°F), pour the lye into the oils and stir with a wooden, plastic or stainless steel spoon.

Grease your selected mould. When the soap reaches trace (see Basic instructions, p27), add the fragrance oil and the jojoba oil and divide the batch into two. Add the colour to one half.

Pour alternately into the mould and swirl with a chopstick or skewer to create a marbled effect. Leave until set.

Turn out of the mould and cut into blocks with a sharp knife or cheesewire. Leave to cure for four weeks.

Carrot, orange and pear salad

Here is another refreshing soap that uses a natural colourant. This soap is enriched with cocoa butter and I have used a 'spiky' pear fragrance oil to add to its deliciousness.

Soap style
Nourishing, with creamy bubbles.

Ingredients
500g (17$^1/_2$ oz) palm oil
500g (17$^1/_2$oz) olive oil
20g ($^3/_4$oz) cocoa butter
130g (4$^1/_2$oz) sodium hydroxide (lye)
375g (13oz) water
5ml (1tsp) liquid carotene
10ml (2tsp) pear fragrance oil

Equipment
Stainless steel or enamel saucepan
Protective glasses
Rubber gloves
Wooden, plastic or stainless steel spoon
2 glass thermometers
Plastic tray or mould of your choice
Sharp knife or cheesewire

Method
Place the palm and olive oils together with the cocoa butter into a stainless steel or enamel saucepan and heat until melted.

Wearing eye protection and rubber gloves, add the sodium hydroxide (lye) to the water and stir. Place a glass thermometer into the oils and the lye solution and when their temperatures both reach 49°C (120°F), pour the lye into the oils and stir with a wooden, plastic or stainless steel spoon.

Grease your mould. When the soap reaches trace (see Basic instructions, p27), add the carotene and fragrance oil and stir. Pour into your selected mould. Leave until set. Turn out of the mould and cut into blocks with a sharp knife or cheesewire. Leave to cure for four weeks.

Right: Olive, mango and jojoba and Carrot, orange and pear salad.

Creamed spinach with bay

Powdered spinach is a good natural colouring that can be bought from herb suppliers. Decorate with a bay leaf.

Soap style
Smooth, enriching and antiseptic.

Ingredients
350g (12oz) coconut oil
350g (12oz) palm oil
200g (7oz) vegetable oil
100g (3¹/₂oz) olive oil
155g (5¹/₂oz) sodium hydroxide (lye)
365g (12¹/₂oz) water
15ml (1tbsp) powdered spinach
5ml (1tsp) vitamin E oil
10ml (2tsp) bay essential oil

Equipment
Stainless steel or enamel saucepan
Protective glasses
Rubber gloves
2 glass thermometers
Wooden, plastic or stainless steel spoon
Plastic tray or mould of your choice
Sharp knife or cheesewire

Method
Place the coconut, palm, vegetable and olive oils into a stainless steel or enamel saucepan and heat until melted. Wearing eye protection and rubber gloves, add the sodium hydroxide (lye) to the water and stir. Place a glass thermometer into the oils and the lye solution and when their temperatures both reach 49°C (120°F), pour the lye into the oils and stir with a wooden, plastic or stainless steel spoon.

Grease your selected mould. When the soap reaches trace (see Basic instructions, p27), add the spinach creamed with a little soap taken from the pot. Then add the vitamin E and essential oil and pour into the mould. Leave until set. Turn out of the mould and cut into blocks with a sharp knife or cheesewire. Leave to cure for four weeks.

Olive, bran and oatmeal loaf

There are times when you need a really scrubby soap to get rid of the dirt and grime. Oatmeal and bran are great for exfoliating.

Soap style
Nourishing and exfoliating.

Ingredients
400g (14oz) coconut oil
350g (12oz) palm oil
250g (3¹/₂oz) olive oil
158g (5¹/₂oz) sodium hydroxide (lye)
365g (12¹/₂oz) water
5ml (1tsp) wheatgerm oil
5ml (1tsp) vitamin E oil
45ml (3tbsp) oatmeal
45ml (3tbsp) bran
10ml (2tsp) essential oil of your choice

Equipment
Stainless steel or enamel saucepan
Protective glasses
Rubber gloves
Wooden, plastic or stainless steel spoon
2 glass thermometers
Plastic tray or mould of your choice
Sharp knife or cheesewire

Method
Place the coconut, palm and olive oils into a stainless steel or enamel saucepan and heat until melted.

Wearing eye protection and rubber gloves, add the sodium hydroxide (lye) to the water and stir. Place a glass thermometer into the oils and the lye solution and when their temperatures both reach 49°C (120°F), pour the lye into the oils and stir with a wooden, plastic or stainless steel spoon.

Grease your selected mould. When the soap reaches trace (see Basic instructions, p27), add the wheatgerm oil and the vitamin E oil and stir. Then add the oatmeal and bran and stir. Finally, stir in the essential oil and pour into your selected mould. Leave until set. Turn out of the mould and cut into blocks with a sharp knife or cheesewire. Leave to cure for four weeks.

Opposite: Creamed spinach with bay and Olive, bran and oatmeal loaf.

French dressing

A super-smooth soap made with the same ingredients as French dressing. Vinegar helps to keep the soap mild, and sugar improves the lather. Mustard helps to unclog pores.

Soap style
Rich, creamy and fruity.

Ingredients
130g (4^1/2oz) olive oil
100g (3^1/2oz) shea butter
145g (5oz) sodium hydroxide (lye)
412g (14^1/2oz) water
15ml (1tbsp) sugar dissolved in 50ml (3^1/2tbsp) water from batch quantity
30ml (2tbsp) mustard powder
10ml (2tsp) cider vinegar
15ml (1tbsp) mustard seeds
5ml (1tsp) lavender essential oil
5ml (1tsp) rosemary essential oil

Equipment
Stainless steel or enamel saucepan
Protective glasses
Rubber gloves
Wooden, plastic or stainless steel spoon
2 glass thermometers
Plastic tray or mould of your choice
Sharp knife or cheesewire

Method
Place the olive oil and shea butter into a stainless steel or enamel saucepan and heat until melted.

Wearing eye protection and rubber gloves, add the sodium hydroxide (lye) to the water and stir. Place a glass thermometer into the oils and the lye solution and when their temperatures both reach 49°C (120°F), pour the lye into the oils and stir with a wooden, plastic or stainless steel spoon.

Grease your selected mould. When the soap reaches trace (see Basic instructions, p27), add the sugar water, mustard powder, cider vinegar and mustard seeds and stir. Then add the essential oils and stir again. Pour into your selected mould. Leave until set. Turn out of the mould and cut into blocks with a sharp knife or cheesewire. Leave to cure for four weeks.

Palm kernel with turmeric

This smart soap is made with a base of palm kernel oil, coloured with a mixture of natural turmeric and liquid chlorophyll.

Soap style
Refreshing, slow bubbles, mildly astringent.

Ingredients
500g (17^1/2oz) palm kernel oil
500g (17^1/2oz) olive oil
2.5ml (^{1}/2tsp) liquid turmeric
2.5ml (^{1}/2tsp) liquid chlorophyll
145g (5oz) sodium hydroxide (lye)
375g (13oz) water
10ml (2tsp) cucumber fragrance oil

Equipment
Stainless steel or enamel saucepan
Protective glasses
Rubber gloves
Wooden, plastic or stainless steel spoon
2 glass thermometers
Plastic tray or mould of your choice
Sharp knife or cheesewire

Method
Place the palm and olive oils into a stainless steel or enamel saucepan and heat until melted.

Mix the turmeric and chlorophyll together. Wearing eye protection and rubber gloves, add the sodium hydroxide (lye) to the water and stir. Place a glass thermometer into the oils and the lye solution and when their temperatures both reach 49°C (120°F), pour the lye into the oils and stir with a wooden, plastic or stainless steel spoon.

Grease your selected mould. When the soap reaches trace (see Basic instructions, p27), add the mixed colours and stir. Then add the fragrance oil and stir. Pour into your selected mould. Leave until set. Turn out of the mould and cut into blocks with a sharp knife or cheesewire. Leave to cure for four weeks.

Opposite: French dressing and Palm kernel with turmeric.

Patisserie

Patisserie is an art form that involves a fine balance of ingredients, colours and textures, as does soapmaking. The main difference is that patisserie feeds the skin from the inside out, whereas soap feeds it from the outside in.

Chocolate lime slice

The first time I made this soap the chocolate layer on the top lifted and cracked slightly; the likeness to chocolate craque icing was indisputable and really added to the overall effect.

Soap style
Creamy chocolate and refreshing lime bubbles – keep away from children!

Ingredients
(quantity listed below makes one layer)
175g (6oz) coconut oil
175g (6oz) vegetable oil
150g (5¼oz) palm oil
187.5g (6½oz) water
74g (2½oz) sodium hydroxide (lye)

(for the chocolate layers)
100g (3½oz) cocoa
2.5ml (½tsp) chocolate fragrance oil

(for the lime layer)
5ml (1tsp) lime fragrance or essential oil
15ml (1tbsp) diluted D & C green 8 pigment powder

Equipment
Stainless steel or enamel saucepan
Whisk
Protective glasses
Rubber gloves
Wooden, plastic or stainless steel spoon
2 glass thermometers
Plastic tray or mould of your choice
Palette knife
Blanket
Sharp knife or cheesewire

Method
Place the coconut, vegetable and palm oils into a stainless steel or enamel saucepan and heat until melted. Add a small amount of warm water to the cocoa and whisk until all the lumps are removed.

Wearing eye protection and rubber gloves, add the sodium hydroxide (lye) to the remaining water and stir. Place a glass thermometer into the oils and the lye solution and when their temperatures both reach 49°C (120°F), pour the lye into the oils and stir with a wooden, plastic or stainless steel spoon. Grease your mould.

While you are waiting for the oils and lye to cool, make up the lime layer.

When the first batch reaches trace (see Basic instructions, p27), add the chocolate fragrance oil and stir. Then fold in the cocoa and stir until it is evenly distributed. Pour the soap into the mould.

Continue with the second batch, but this time add the lime essential oil and colouring instead of the chocolate fragrance and cocoa. When the soap reaches trace, pour it carefully over the chocolate layer. Leave it to set for at least 2 hours.

Now make an identical batch of chocolate soap as described and pour it over the lime layer. Use a palette knife to make swirls on the surface so that it looks like icing.

Cover it with a blanket and leave for 48 hours or until hard. Turn out of the mould and cut into blocks with a sharp knife or cheesewire. Leave to cure for four weeks.

Passion fruit cake

The addition of rosehip seed and passion flower oil gives this soap a wonderfully smooth, creamy texture. A little ylang ylang and black pepper essential oils add a touch of pure wickedness to this luxurious soap!

Soap style
Hard and long-lasting. Smooth, creamy and nourishing for the skin.

Ingredients
458g (16oz) coconut oil
350g (12oz) palm oil
177g (6oz) olive oil
160g (5^1/$_2$oz) sodium hydroxide (lye)
369g (13oz) water
10ml (2tsp) rosehip seed oil
5ml (1tsp) passion flower oil
15ml (1tbsp) ylang ylang essential oil
2.5ml (^{1}/$_2$ tsp) medium ultramarine pigment
 powder
A tiny pinch (the tip of a teaspoon) D & C Red 33
 pigment powder

Equipment
Stainless steel or enamel saucepan
Protective glasses
Rubber gloves
Wooden, plastic or stainless steel spoon
2 glass thermometers
Plastic tray or mould of your choice
2 plastic or glass jugs
Blanket
Sharp knife or cheesewire

Opposite: Passion fruit cake and Strawberry and banana gateau.

Method
Place the coconut, palm and olive oils into a stainless steel or enamel saucepan and heat until melted. Wearing eye protection and rubber gloves, add the sodium hydroxide (lye) to the water and stir.

Place a glass thermometer into the oils and the lye solution and when their temperatures both reach 49°C (120°F), pour the lye into the oils and stir with a wooden, plastic or stainless steel spoon. Grease a square plastic tray (or line a cardboard box with a dustbin bag) to use as a mould.

When the soap reaches light trace (see Basic instructions, p27), add the rosehip seed and passion flower and essential oils and stir. Divide the batch equally into two jugs.

Mix the blue and red pigment powders together. Add 45ml (3tbsp) of warm water and stir. Pour the diluted colourant into one of the jugs of soap and stir thoroughly. Pour the uncoloured batch of soap into the mould and set aside.

Continue to stir the coloured batch until it has fully traced, then gently pour it over the soap in the mould. Cover the soap with a blanket and leave for 48 hours or until hard. Cut into blocks with a sharp knife or cheesewire. Leave to cure for four weeks.

Strawberry and banana gateau

This yummy strawberry and banana gateau is a combination of cold-processed and melt and pour soaps. To make it look even more like sponge cake, you could try adding some loofah particles to the banana soap mix.

Soap style

Fruity, creamy, bubbly – and definitely not edible.

Ingredients

(for the banana soap)
350g (12¼oz) coconut oil
300g (10½oz) palm oil
350g (12¼oz) vegetable oil
148g (5½oz) sodium hydroxide (lye)
375g (13oz) water
175g (6oz) goat's milk (slightly warmed)
15ml (1tbsp) ground loofah (optional)
15ml (1tbsp) banana fragrance
15ml (1tbsp) diluted annatto powder

(for the topping)
500g (1lb) clear glycerine soap base
2.5ml (½tsp) strawberry fragrance oil
Red liquid food colouring
Witch hazel

Equipment

Stainless steel or enamel saucepan
Protective glasses
Rubber gloves
Wooden, plastic or stainless steel spoon
2 glass thermometers
Whisk
Banana candle mould or mould of your choice
Sharp knife
Plastic or glass jug
Cling film

Method

Place the coconut, palm and vegetable oils into a stainless steel or enamel saucepan and heat until melted.

Wearing eye protection and rubber gloves, add sodium hydroxide (lye) to the water and stir. Place a glass thermometer into the oils and the lye solution and when their temperatures both reach 49°C (120°F), pour the lye into the oils. Then add the warm goat's milk. Stir with a wooden, plastic or stainless steel spoon. The goat's milk does tend to curdle. If this happens, whisk furiously with a hand whisk or a hand-held blender. Also, don't worry about the orange colour or the smell of ammonia – both of these disappear quite quickly, leaving a wonderful soap.

When the soap reaches light trace (see Basic instructions, p27), pour about half a cup into a banana-shaped mould (you don't need to fill it up, as you only need a few slices for decoration). Add the loofah (if required), the banana fragrance oil and the annatto to the remaining soap and stir thoroughly. Pour it into the mould and leave to set for about 48 hours.

When the soap in the banana mould is hard, take it out and slice it. For added effect, score the surface of each slice with a sharp knife so that it truly looks like a banana slice.

To make the strawberry topping, cut the soap base into rough chunks and place them in a plastic or glass jug. Stand the jug in a saucepan half-full of water and place on the stove. Heat the water until the soap begins to melt in the jug. Keeping the heat as low as possible, cover the saucepan. When the soap has completely melted, add the strawberry fragrance oil and the red colouring. Stir these in gently to avoid making air bubbles. Wipe the surface of the banana soap with witch hazel, then pour the strawberry soap over the top. Arrange the slices of banana on the surface. Leave to set, then cut into blocks. Cover with cling film. Leave to cure for four weeks.

Peppermint cream

Peppermint is one of the essential oils that stands up really well to the soapmaking process. The essential oil is a stimulant and neither the soap or the oil should be used during the first three months of pregnancy. That aside, if you want a really refreshing 'buzzy' bar of soap, you can't do better than this one.

Soap style
Hard and long-lasting, with big bubbles. Invigorating!

Ingredients
450g (16oz) coconut oil
450g (16oz) palm oil
100g (3$^{1}/_{2}$oz) olive oil
100g white beeswax
160g (5$^{1}/_{2}$oz) sodium hydroxide (lye)
412 g (14$^{1}/_{2}$oz) water
15ml (1tbsp) peppermint essential oil
2.5ml ($^{1}/_{2}$tsp) chromium oxide pigment

Equipment
Stainless steel or enamel saucepan
Protective glasses
Rubber gloves
Wooden, plastic or stainless steel spoon
2 glass thermometers
Plastic tray or mould of your choice
2 glass or plastic jugs
Wooden chopstick or kebab skewer
Sharp knife or cheesewire

Method
Place the coconut, palm and olive oils with the beeswax in a stainless steel or enamel saucepan and heat until melted. Wearing eye protection and rubber gloves, add the sodium hydroxide (lye) to the water and stir.

Place a glass thermometer into the oils and the lye solution and when their temperatures both reach 49°C (120°F) pour the lye into the oils and stir with a wooden, plastic or stainless steel spoon. Grease a square plastic tray (or line a cardboard box with a dustbin bag) to use as a mould.

When the soap reaches light trace (see Basic instructions, p27), add the essential oil and stir. Divide the batch equally into two jugs. Pour the diluted colourant into one of the jugs of soap and stir thoroughly.

Pour the soaps alternately into the mould and swirl with a wooden chopstick or skewer. Cover the soap with a blanket and leave for 48 hours or until hard. Cut into blocks with a sharp knife or cheesewire. Leave to cure for four weeks before use.

Flower fancies

The beauty of melt and pour glycerine soap is that you can place so many different things in it. These pretty gift soaps were made in 10 minutes, using the tray from an empty box of biscuits as a mould. You could also make the soap in small individual jelly moulds or pour the soap into an oblong food container and cut around them with a cookie cutter. The flowers are made from silk so they will retain their bright colours.

Soap style
These pretty, decorative soaps will astound your friends.

Ingredients
1kg (2lb) clear glycerine soap base
5ml (1tsp) fragrance or essential oil of your choice

Equipment
Sharp knife
Stainless steel or enamel saucepan
Plastic or glass jug
Wooden, plastic or stainless steel spoon
Plastic tray or mould of your choice
6 silk flower heads
Toothpick

Method
Cut the soap base into rough chunks and place them in a plastic or glass jug. Stand the jug in a saucepan half-full of water and place on the stove. Heat the water until the soap begins to melt in the jug. Keeping the heat as low as possible, cover the saucepan. When the soap has completely melted, add the fragrance or essential oil of your choice. Stir this in gently to avoid air bubbles.

Pour the soap into the mould. Trim the flower heads, so there are no sharp stems to scratch you. While the soaps are still liquid push one or two flowers gently into the centre of each one with a toothpick. Make sure they are completely submerged. Leave to set (place in the fridge if you are in a hurry). When hard, turn the soaps over and push them out of the moulds. Trim off any rough edges with a sharp knife.

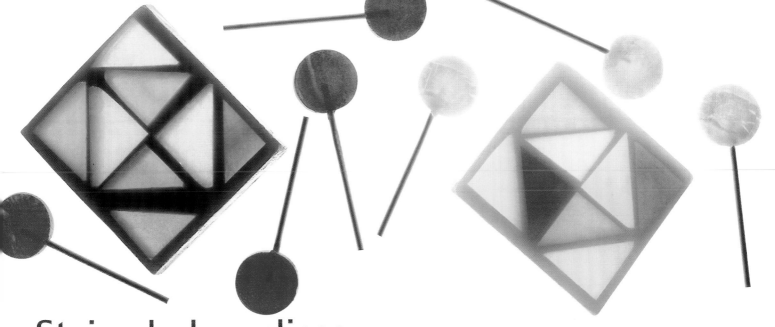

Stained glass slices

These clever soaps were created by British soapmaker, Glenys Pople. The coloured micas give the glass panels a glittery effect. She has given the recipe from scratch, but the technique also offers a useful way to use up oddments of coloured glycerine soaps.

Soap style

Glittery and multi-coloured. Wonderful show-off soaps for the bathroom.

Ingredients

1600g (3lb 8oz) transparent glycerine soap base

White, gold, copper, wisteria, crimson and sapphire mica (enough of each to fit the tip of a teaspoon)

Either 2.5ml (^{1}/2tsp) water-dispersible titanium dioxide for the white version, or 1ml (^{1}/8tsp) titanium dioxide and 2.5ml (^{1}/2tsp) black oxide for the black version

2.5ml (^{1}/2tsp) essential oil of your choice

Equipment

Sharp knife or cheesewire

Plastic or glass jug

Stainless steel or enamel saucepan

Moulds: 60cm (24in) of 65mm (2^1/2in) PVC pipe, square, cut into six 10cm (4in) lengths, ends sealed with packing tape

Rectangular baking tray

Method

Take 1000g of the soap base and set aside. Divide the remaining soap base into six equal portions. Melt each of the six portions in turn by placing them in a plastic or glass jug. Stand the jug in a saucepan half-full of water and place on the stove. Heat the water until the soap begins to melt in the jug. Keeping the heat as low as possible, cover the saucepan. When the soap has melted, colour each with one of the micas: white, gold, crimson, wisteria, copper and sapphire.

Pour into the PVC moulds that you have sealed, one colour to each, and leave at room temperature until they have set. Don't worry about any bubbles that form on the top.

Take out of the moulds. Cut each square of soap across the diagonal to make four triangles, then cut each of these into two equal-sized triangles, to make eight pieces. You can cut them into smaller triangles if you want.

Arrange the triangles in your baking tray so that they form a pattern for six soaps (see photograph). You can use your imagination here. Make sure you leave a small gap between each of the triangles and a wider gap round the edges and between each group.

Now make the overpour. Melt the remaining base and colour with 2.5ml (^{1}/2tsp) water-dispersible titanium dioxide. Alternatively, for the black version, melt the remaining base and colour it with 1ml (^{1}/8tsp) titanium dioxide and 2.5ml (^{1}/2tsp) black oxide. Experiment to get the colour you want, mixing the black oxide and titanium dioxide with 5ml (1tsp) of hot water. Add 2.5ml (^{1}/2tsp) essential oil of your choice.

When the soap reaches 54°C (130°F), pour over the triangle arrangements, taking care to fill all the spaces. Allow to cool overnight. Remove from the mould and cut into six soaps. Trim the soaps until their surfaces are level. If not using immediately, wrap in cling film.

Silk and shea butter Christmas cake

This luxury soap can truly be described as having the smoothness of silk, since that's just what it contains! I have used mica in two different ways, firstly, in the oils to slightly colour the soap, and secondly, to add glitter to the surface. Frankincense and myrrh are traditional Christmas fragrances, but they are quite expensive. You can, of course, replace these with your own favourite essentials.

Soap style
Wildly extravagant, silky and heady.

Ingredients
450g (16oz) coconut oil
350g (12oz) palm oil
200g (7oz) olive oil
100g (3^1/$_2$oz) shea butter
10ml (2tsp) copper mica
166g (5^3/$_4$oz) sodium hydroxide (lye)
412g (14^1/$_2$oz) water
15ml (1tbsp) cut raw silk fibres
5ml (1tsp) frankincense essential oil
5ml (1tsp) myrrh essential oil
10ml (2tsp) cocoa powder
1ml (^{1}/$_8$tsp) gold mica

Equipment
Stainless steel or enamel saucepan
Protective glasses
Rubber gloves
Wooden, plastic or stainless steel spoon
2 glass thermometers
Plastic tray or mould of your choice
2 glass or plastic jugs
Wooden chopstick or kebab skewer
Blanket
Sharp knife or cheesewire

Method
Place the coconut, palm and olive oils and shea butter in a stainless steel or enamel saucepan and heat until melted. Add the copper mica. Wearing eye protection and rubber gloves, add the sodium hydroxide (lye) to the water and stir. Add the silk fibres to the lye solution and stir until they have completely dissolved.

Place a glass thermometer into the oils and the lye solution and when their temperatures both reach 49°C (120°F), pour the lye into the oils and stir with a wooden, plastic or stainless steel spoon. Grease a square plastic tray (or line a cardboard box with a dustbin bag) to use as a mould.

When the soap reaches light trace (see Basic instructions, p27), add the essential oils and stir. Divide the batch equally into two jugs.

Blend the cocoa into a cream with a few drops of warm water. Pour this into one of the jugs of soap and stir until it is evenly distributed. Pour the soaps into the mould alternately and swirl with a wooden chopstick or kebab skewer.

When the soap is still tacky, put a tiny amount of gold mica onto the tip of a teaspoon and blow it over the surface of the soap. Repeat until the mica is used up.

Cover the soap with a blanket and leave for 48 hours or until hard. Cut into blocks with a sharp knife or cheesewire. Leave to cure for four weeks before use.

Petit fours

This section includes those after-dinner delights that depend on presentation as much as ingredients. The way you finish, package and present your soaps says a lot about you and your sense of style. Of course, if you prefer fish and chips to caviar, there is no reason why you shouldn't use cleverly folded newspaper to wrap your soaps. The important thing is to make the soaps your own.

Lime loofah

For an exfoliating delight, try filling a loofah with your favourite soap. You can do this in one of two ways. The first is to cut the top off the loofah, wrap it in cling film and fill the core with soap. Then cut into circular slices. Alternatively, to achieve the effect you see here, cut the loofah in half, remove the core, wrap the outside with cling film, securing the ends with tape, and fill the indentation with soap. The first method is perhaps prettier, but the second gives you a more practical soap, with loofah on one side and soap on the other.

Soap style
A refreshing, scrubby pleasure.

Ingredients
350g (12^1/$_2$oz) coconut oil
300g (10^1/$_2$oz) palm oil
350g (12^1/$_4$oz) vegetable oil
148g (5^1/$_2$oz) sodium hydroxide (lye)
375g (13oz) water
1 large loofah
15ml (1tbsp) lime essential oil
15ml (1tbsp) diluted D & C green 8
   pigment powder

Equipment
Stainless steel or enamel saucepan
Protective glasses
Rubber gloves
Wooden, plastic or stainless steel spoon
2 glass thermometers
Cling film
Blanket
Sharp serrated knife

Method
Place the coconut, palm and vegetable oils into a stainless steel or enamel saucepan and heat until melted.

Wearing eye protection and rubber gloves, add sodium hydroxide (lye) to the water and stir. Place a glass thermometer into the oils and the lye solution and when their temperatures both reach 49°C (120°F), pour the lye into the oils and stir.

Prepare your loofah as described above. When the soap reaches light trace (see Basic instructions, p27), add the lime essential oil and the colouring and stir thoroughly. When the soap reaches heavy trace, pour it into the loofah halves. Cover the soap with a blanket and leave for 48 hours or until it is hard.

Cut the loofah into slices with a sharp serrated knife. Leave to cure for four weeks before use.

Jasmine cream

Unless you are a millionaire, you are unlikely to want to put pure jasmine essential oil into your soap. However, there are some wonderful delicate fragrance oils that do credit to this beautiful flower. You can also buy dried jasmine flowers, but they tend to look rather sad, so I have settled here for a simple swirled pale yellow and white soap.

Soap style
Traditionally feminine, creamy romantic soap to use before that night at the opera.

Ingredients
350g (12^1/$_4$oz) coconut oil
300g (10^1/$_2$oz) palm oil
350g (12^1/$_4$oz) vegetable oil
50g (2oz) shea butter
50g (2oz) white beeswax
158g (5^1/$_2$oz) sodium hydroxide (lye)
412g (14^1/$_2$oz) water
15ml (1tbsp) jasmine fragrance oil
2ml (^{1}/$_4$tsp) diluted quinoline yellow pigment

Equipment
Stainless steel or enamel saucepan
Protective glasses
Rubber gloves
Wooden, plastic or stainless steel spoon
2 glass thermometers
Mould of your choice
Wooden chopstick or kebab skewer
Blanket
Sharp knife or cheesewire
Pastry cutter

Method
Place the coconut, palm and vegetable oils together with the shea butter and beeswax into a stainless steel or enamel saucepan and heat until melted.

Wearing eye protection and rubber gloves, add the sodium hydroxide (lye) to the water and stir. Place a glass thermometer into the oils and the lye solution and when their temperatures both reach 49°C (120°F), pour the lye into the oils and stir with a wooden, plastic or stainless steel spoon.

Grease your selected mould. When the soap reaches light trace (see Basic instructions, p27), add the fragrance oil and divide the batch in two. Add the colour to one batch and stir. Pour alternately into the mould and swirl with a chopstick or skewer to create a marbled effect.

Cover the soap with a blanket and leave for 48 hours or until hard. Turn out of mould and cut into blocks with a sharp knife or cheesewire. Trim the edges with a serrated pastry cutter. Leave to cure for four weeks before use.

Soap balls

These soaps make great gifts.

Cold-processed soap that is only a day old is still soft and, provided you wear rubber gloves, you can form it into balls in the same way that you make dumplings. You can also melt grated soap in a pot with just enough water to dampen it and squidge the result into balls in the same way. When you have made your balls, wet the surface and roll them in dried herbs or flower petals.

Soap biscuits

These elegant little soaps are ideal for guests.

You can buy cocktail-sized cookie cutters in a wide variety of shapes and use them to cut your soaps into guest-size bars. Top the soaps with flowers, shells, nuts or seeds, and pile them up in a pretty dish.

Sweethearts

You can embed decorative items on the surface of your soap by pressing them in before the soap gets too hard.

These little hearts are made from off-cuts of ready-made soap and are ideal to decorate soaps for the love in your life. You could also decorate the soap with shapes cut from fired terracotta clay. There are also various clays on the market that will harden when heated in a normal domestic oven. These come in a selection of colours, or you can use a natural colour and paint them. You could also personalize your soap by cutting out initials.

Soap beads

If you are going to a special dinner party, then you should be doing everything possible to show off your soapmaking skills, and what better way than to wear your own exquisitely fragranced soap beads? This is also a very canny way of using up all those off-cuts.

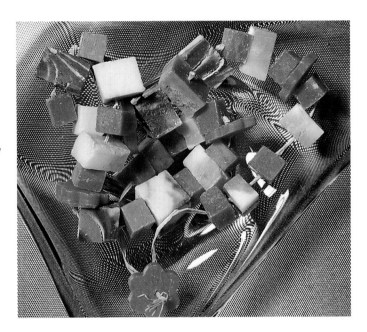

You can cut your soap into small blocks or circles, or mould it into balls. Make a hole through the centre of each with a fine knitting needle. Then, using a sharp needle, thread them on to nylon thread or natural raffia. Intersperse your soap beads with shells or flower heads (silk or dried), and you'll have a unique talking piece at the dinner table.

Fresh fruit

A basket of soap 'fruit' is a fun birthday gift.

Latex moulds are fine for use in both cold process and melt and pour soapmaking. Simply add the appropriate fragrance and colour to your favourite soap mix and pour into the mould until it has set. You can also make gold cupids in a latex mould: just add some gold mica to a melt and pour base before filling the mould.

A la carte

There are numerous ways to make bathtime a sensuous experience without paying fortunes for shop-bought luxuries. In this section, you will find interesting bathtime items to make while you are waiting for your soap to trace. They also make delightful gifts to include with your soap.

Bath fizzer

One of the fun parts of this recipe is finding a suitable mould. Small fizzy balls can be made with meatball tongs (if you can find them), or you can cut a hollow ball into two halves and use them to make large 'bombs'. Any mould will do, but take into account the fact that you need to dry the fizzers out in an oven set to minimum heat. Be careful not to use excess colouring. I once turned a customer and his bath and towel bright pink by overcolouring a sample fizzer.

Soap style
Explosive and great fun.

Ingredients
495g (1lb 1¹/2oz) baking soda
495g (1lb 1¹/2oz) citric acid
5ml (1tsp) essential oil of your choice
3 drops liquid food colouring
Witch hazel

Equipment
Wooden, stainless steel or plastic spoon
Fine spray gun or atomizer
Hollow ball cut in half
Bun tray

Method
Thoroughly mix the dry ingredients, then add the essential oil and colouring. Carefully spray the mixture with witch hazel whilst mixing it with your hands. You want the consistency of damp sand, but if you add too much witch hazel your mixture will fizz. With half a ball in each hand, scoop up the mixture and clamp the two halves tightly together. Carefully remove the ball from around the fizzer, putting it into the bun tray (this takes practice – if it falls apart, the mixture wasn't wet enough!). Put the bun tray in the oven at the lowest setting with the door open for about ten minutes or until the fizzers are rock-hard.

Rosemary sea salt scrub

This is a truly decadent delight that should leave your skin glowing and refreshed. If you want an extra buzz, get your partner to apply it before you have a shared bath. You need to store this in a wide-necked jar so you can scoop out a handful easily.

Soap style
Naughty but nice.

Ingredients
100g (3¹/₂oz) your favourite handmade soap grated
100g (3¹/₂oz) sweet almond oil infused with rosemary
200g (7oz) coarse sea salt
2.5ml (¹/₂tsp) rosemary essential oil

Equipment
Cheese grater
Double boiler or bowl and saucepan
Wide-necked jar with screw-top lid

Method
Put the soap and almond oil in a double boiler (or a bowl standing in a saucepan of water) and melt over a low heat. Place the salt and essential oil in a wide-necked jar. Pour the melted oils over the top. Do not use the scrub until it is completely cold.

Camomile, honey and vitamin E lotion bar

Use this bar to moisturize dry skin and to protect your skin from chapping. If you can acquire a push-up container all the better, otherwise you can use tin boxes or old cosmetic jars and apply the lotion with your fingertips.

Style
Soothing and moisturizing.

Ingredients
28g (1oz) beeswax
28g (1oz) shea butter
28g (1oz) mango or cocoa butter
28g (1oz) sweet almond oil
5ml (1tsp) honey
2.5ml (^{1}/$_2$tsp) vitamin E oil
2 drops Roman camomile essential oil

Equipment
Double boiler or bowl and saucepan
Wooden, stainless steel or plastic spoon
Push-up containers, tin boxes or jars

Method
Melt the beeswax, shea and mango (or cocoa) butter in a double boiler (or a bowl standing in a saucepan of water) together with the almond oil using a low heat. Stir in the honey and the vitamin E oil. Stir in the essential oil. Pour into containers and put in the fridge to harden.

Right: Camomile, honey and vitamin E lotion bar and Chocolate after-dinner mint lip smacker.

Chocolate after-dinner mint lip smacker

Now that you have a soft and fragrant body, you'll want to make sure you don't spoil the effect with dry, sore lips. Solve the problem with this delicious lip balm. Push-up tubes can be bought on the internet, but if you have a problem finding them, fill a lidded jar with the balm and smooth it on with your fingers.

Style
Yummy and soothing, you won't know how you lived without it.

Ingredients
10ml (2tsp) melted beeswax
10ml (2tsp) melted cocoa butter
10ml (2tsp) sweet almond oil
5ml (1tsp) shea butter
4ml (¾tsp) cocoa
4 drops honey
2.5ml (½tsp) vitamin E oil
1 drop peppermint essential oil

Equipment
Double boiler or bowl and saucepan
Wooden, stainless steel or plastic spoon
Push-up tubes or jars

Method
Melt the beeswax, shea, cocoa butter and almond oil in a double boiler (or a bowl standing in a saucepan of water) over a low heat. Add the cocoa and stir. Stir in the honey and the vitamin E oil. Add the peppermint essential oil. Pour into containers and put in the fridge to harden.

Bathroom freshener

There are times when your bathroom may not smell quite as fragrant as you do. Happily, with all these new essential and fragrance oils around, it is very easy to make up your own remedy.

All you need in addition to the fragrance is a pack of plain gelatine, some vegetable colouring and a container (glass tumblers or baby food jars are ideal). Follow the instructions on the gelatine pack, but instead of adding edibles, add a teaspoonful of your favourite essential oil and a few drops of colouring. Leave to set. Pierce a few holes in the lid of the jar and place in the offending area. If using a tumbler, cover with cling film pierced with holes.

The tip

Soap style

Gives the kids a reason to wash! NB: not for small children, as they could swallow the coins.

Ingredients

1kg (2lb) clear glycerine soap base
New clean coins
5ml (1tsp) fragrance or essential oil
  of your choice

Equipment

Sharp knife
Plastic or glass jug
Stainless steel or enamel saucepan
Wooden, stainless steel or plastic spoon
Mould of your choice

Method

Cut the soap base into rough chunks and place them in a plastic or glass jug. Stand the jug in a saucepan half-full of water and place it on the stove over a low heat. Keeping the heat as low as possible, cover the saucepan. When the soap has completely melted, add the fragrance or essential oil and stir gently. Pour the melted soap into a mould of your choice and simply drop in the coins.

After-dinner entertainment

By the time you have worked your way through this book, you should have lots of wonderfully coloured and fragranced soap scraps left. These may appear to be too small to do anything constructive with, but if you are crafty you can actually make great mosaics with them.

If you have ever tried using proper mosaic tiles, you will know that they are hard to cut. Soap, on the other hand, is easy to cut into tiny tiles and, what's more, you can stick them to paper by just roughing or scoring the back of the tiles and wetting them.

Draw your own design or glue an existing picture or photograph onto a piece of rigid card or board. Select and cut your pieces of soap, keeping them an even thickness. Score and wet the back of each piece and push it firmly down onto the picture.

If the finished picture is left in a very dry environment, you may find the tiles will lift in time. One solution is to spray the picture every now and then with a fine mist. Alternatively, hang the picture in the bathroom, where the steam should help to keep it damp.

You could also mosaic the top of a jewellery box or work on any surface that allows you to apply paper. Would the first person who makes a mirror frame please send me a photograph of it!

The soap biz

After the publication of *The Handmade Soap Book*, I was inundated with enquiries from soapmakers who wanted to turn their hobby into a small business. This really isn't as easy as it seems, and one particular lady left me feeling mortified. Inspired by my book, she had gone out and bought herself a whole field of goats, with the intention of setting up a goat's milk soap business. After talking to me, she realized that she did not have the resources to sell her soap legally. There are strict requirements that have to be fulfilled.

To put matters straight, I will set out all the things you should consider before setting up your own soap business. Having run one myself for several years, I can promise you great job satisfaction, though sadly, as with any business based on a traditional craft, it will seldom provide great financial rewards.

Unfortunately for the hobby soapmaker, the laws in Europe governing soap are extremely stringent, as they fall under the same legislation as cosmetics. This is very hard on the small soapmaker as, in order to sell your soap, you need to be prepared to make a considerable financial investment. In the USA, soap is classified as a 'detergent', and many of these restrictions do not apply.

The following European rules apply whether you are selling your products at a small craft fair or to a gigantic retail chain. Before you accept money for your product, you must ensure that you have followed all the rules and regulations. If you have any doubts or queries, contact your local trading standards officer.

Weights and measures

Trading standards require you to accurately weigh your product and to display the weight on all your packaging. To do this, you will need 'stamped for trade' scales. You can purchase both new and reconditioned scales from specialist companies, which you will find in your local telephone trade directory. Be sure that your supplier realizes that they must meet trading standards regulations.

Soap loses moisture over time, so it is difficult to state a weight on your bar that will remain accurate over a long period of time. The good news is that you have a 4 per cent allowance either way. It is wise, though, to ensure your soap is 10 per cent heavier than the stated weight, and to label it as 'average net weight' rather than be precise.

Although many people seem to sell soap 'by the inch' or some other measurement, this is illegal. Soap should be sold strictly by weight.

Pigments

When using man-made pigments in your soapmaking, you will need to ensure that they have been approved for cosmetic use. Ask for written assurances from your supplier.

You can use natural herbs and spices to colour your soap, but you may not use candle dyes, wax crayons or many of the dyes formulated for textiles. Your labelling must display the 'CI' number of the colourant that you have used. Your supplier should be able to provide this.

Labelling

To ensure that people of all nationalities can identify the ingredients in soap and cosmetics, each ingredient is designated an INCI name, and this must be used on your labels. A full directory of INCIs can be found at http://dg3.eudra.org/inci/incif1.htm.

Essential oils should be described by their Latin names, 'water' should be called 'aqua', and fragrance oils should be referred to as 'parfum'.

Ingredient information should be headed 'ingredients' and listed in order of quantity. So if there is more water in your soap than anything else, start your list with 'aqua'. It is not necessary to list 'sodium hydroxide' as an ingredient as, if you have made your soap correctly, it no longer exists in the cured bar. When working with ready-made soap bases, make sure that you get a full list of ingredients from your supplier.

You must also include a batch number indicating the date the soap was made. If any problems arise, you will then be able to trace the batch back to your records.

If your soap looks particularly edible, it is necessary to state 'Soap, do not eat' on your label.

On some occasions your presentation will make it impossible for you to display full ingredients on each bar. In these circumstances, you are allowed to show the ingredients on a display card at the point of sale. Your soap label should also include contact details for the manufacturer. Your name and postcode will be sufficient.

Record keeping

By law you must keep very accurate records for each batch of soaps you make. These are referred to in the industry as P.I.Ps (Product Information Packs). Each pack should contain your recipe, data sheets for all your ingredients, batch numbers and dates of manufacture. If you deal with good suppliers, they will provide these.

Keep accurate notes of any problems that occur during the soapmaking procedure.

Responsible person

This is the really tough one... every batch of soap you make for sale must be 'signed off' by a pharmacist or a toxicologist. Whilst there is no law that requires you to have your soap tested, your 'responsible person' will require the precise detail

in your P.I.P. to confirm that your soaps are safe. Ensure that the person you use has full insurance cover.

Insurance

You are not required by law to take out product liability insurance, but you should do this. It only takes one person to blame your soap for the rash on their hands and, rightly or wrongly, you could find yourself facing a huge debt in legal fees. A general insurance broker will be able to supply you with business insurance.

Environmental issues

As if the above is not prohibitive enough, at the time of writing legislation relating to your premises is under consideration. If it is adopted, you will require a licence for your workshop, and this will cost several thousand pounds a year. The Department of the Environment will be able to give you more up-to-date information on this.

Place of manufacture

Before selling your soap you must write to the Department of Trade and Industry and inform them of your address and of the fact that soap is being manufactured on your premises.

Stockists and resources

UK

Internet resources
http://users.silverlink.net/~timer/soapdesign.html
Formulas and tips.

www.handmadesoap.co.uk
General information.
www.handmadesoap.co.uk
(go to the soapmakers section)
www.the-sage.com
Saponification software.

INCI LIST
http://dg3.eudra.org/inci/incif1.htm

Base oils
William Hodgson & Co
73a London Road
Alderley Edge
Cheshire SK9 7DX
Tel: 01625 599111
*Coconut, palm, vegetable, etc
(minimum 12.5 kilo block).*

Statfold Seed Oil Development
Statfold Barn Farm
Ashby Road, Tamworth
Staffordshire B79 0BV
Tel: 01827 830871

FPI Sales Ltd
Meadow Park Industrial Estate
Essendine
Stamford
Linconshire PE9 4LT
Tel: 01780 482200
info@fpisales.com
Glycerine soap base.

Essential and fragrance oils
Essentially Oils
8 Mount Farm
Junction Road
Churchill, Chipping Norton
Oxfordshire OX7 6NP
Tel: 01608 659544
essentially.oils.ltd@dial.pipex.com
Also sell cosmetic clays.

Butterbur & Sage Ltd
7 Tessa Rd
Reading
Berkshire RG1 8HH
Tel: 01189 505100
*Also sell cosmetic ingredients such as beeswax,
cocoa butter, etc.*

Naturania Aromatherapy
Llysaeron
Penrhyncoch
Aberystwyth
Wales SY23 3EP
Tel: 01970 820858
naturania@btinternet.com
Wonderful essential oil blends.

Herbs, dried flowers and cosmetic ingredients
Neals Yard Remedies
2 Neals Yard
Covent Garden
London WC2H 9DP
Tel: 0207 3797222

Herbal Apothecary
103 High Street
Syston
Leicester LE7 1GQ
Tel: 0116 2602690

Cosmetic pigments & oxides
The Handmade Soap Company Ltd
20 & 21 Llambed Business Park
Lampeter
Ceredigion SA48 8LT
Tel: 01570 423585
Mail order only - no callers please.

Other equipment
La Cuisiniere
81/83 and 87 Northcote Road
London SW11 6PL
Tel: 020 7223 4409
Fax: 020 7924 4466
Email: lacuisiniere@virgin.net
Glass thermometers and cooking utensils.

CANADA/US

Internet resources
http://www.mindspring.com/~sugrplum
Soap supplies, software and chat room.

http://nwselp.epcc.edu/elp/tempconv.html
*Temperature converter (from centigrade to
fahrenheit or fahrenheit to centigrade).*

http://www.sweetcakes.com
*This address will take you to Linda Jines' site where
her wonderful fragrance oils are listed and can be
bought by credit card.*

General
www.sugarplum.net
www.rainbowmeadow.com
www.glorybee.com
www.from-nature-with-love.com

Martin Creative Moulds
PO Box 101
Black Creek BC V9J1K8
http://www.martincreative.com.
Moulds.
Milky Way Molds
PMB473
4326 Woodstock
Portland OR 97206
www.milkywaymolds.com
Moulds.

Rainbow Meadow
6943 Clarklake Rd
Jackson MI 49201
Tel: 517-764-4170
e-mail: rainbow@sojourn.com
Essential oils, palm and coconut, jojoba, avocado.

Sun Feather Soapmaking Supply
HCR 84 Box 60-A
Potsdam NY 13676
Tel: 800-771-7627
Lye, fats, soap fragrance, soap colour.

Sweet Cakes Soapmaking Supplies
Linda Jines, Proprietor
39 Brookdale Road
Bloomfield NJ 07003
Tel: 201-338-9830
Fragrance oils.

'The Pigment Lady'
Lori Schenkelberg
1035 Dulaney Mill Drive
Frederick MD 21702
*Cosmetic pigments, oxides, colour information
and moulds.*

Bibliography
Failor, Catherine, *Making Natural Liquid Soap*,
  Storey Publishing
Failor, Catherine, *Making Transparent Soap*,
  Storey Publishing
Miller Cavitch, Susan, *The Soapmaker's Companion*,
  Storey Publishing (Cassell)
White, Elaine C, *Soap Recipes*, Valley Hills Press
Worwood, Valerie Ann, *The Fragrant Pharmacy*,
  Bantam

Index

acne 22, 23
additives 15, 17–18
After-dinner entertainment 76
ageing skin 17, 22, 23
allergies 15, 17, 18, 20
ammonia smell 8, 62
antibacterial properties 17
antidepressant properties 22, 23
anti-fungal properties 22, 23
antioxidant properties 17, 18
antiseptic properties 22, 23, 54
aphrodisiac properties 23
astringent properties 17, 23,
    49, 57
Avocado melt 44

Bath fizzer 72
Bathroom freshener 75
Bucks fizz 36

Camomile, honey and vitamin E
    lotion bar 74
Carrot, orange and pear salad 53
caustic soda *see* sodium hydroxide
chapped skin 15, 17
Chocolate after-dinner mint lip
    smacker 75
Chocolate lime slice 58
cold-process: method 10, 27
    re-batching 11, 26
    recipes 34, 36, 40, 44, 46, 48, 49,
    50, 52, 53, 54, 57, 58, 61, 62, 63,
    66, 67, 68
colour fade 10, 25
colourings 24–5
    adding 8, 27
    for commercial soapmaking 77
    in re-batch 26
    stockists 79
commercial soapmaking 7, 77–8
cosmetic pigments 24, 25, 77
    stockists 79
Creamed spinach
    with bay 54
Creamy lavender 50
Crème de menthe 33
curdling 8, 11, 62
curing 9–10
cutting 13, 14

deodorizing properties 17, 22, 33
dermatitis 22, 23
disinfectant properties 15
Dock, nettle and lemongrass pâté 48
dry skin 15, 17, 23, 74

eczema 15, 17, 22, 23
emollient properties 17
equipment 13–14
    cleaning 12, 14
essential oils 20, 22–3, 77
    combining 22
    stockists 79
exfoliation 15, 17, 23, 26, 48, 54, 67

fillers 8, 17, 23, 26, 27
fixatives for fragrances 15, 17, 20, 23
Flower fancies 64
flowers: dried 17, 50
    silk 64
fragrance oils 20, 22–3, 77
    adding 8, 27
    in re-batch 26
    stockists 79
    synthetic 30
French dressing 57
Fresh fruit 71
fresh ingredients 15, 17, 20, 26, 48
fruity soaps 34, 36, 39, 44, 52, 53, 58,
    61, 62, 67, 71

glycerine 10, 15, 17, 24, 25, 27, 28
    see also melt and pour
goat's milk 8, 24, 26, 62, 77
greasy skin 17, 22, 23

Handmade Soap Book, The
    (Melinda Coss) 7, 77
Handmade Paper Book, The
    (Angela Ramsay) 28
hardening *see* setting
healing properties 15, 20
herbs 17, 48, 54

ingredients 15–18
insect repellent properties 22, 23, 26
internet 7, 15, 75, 79

Jasmine cream 68

labelling regulations 77–8
layered soaps 26, 34, 42, 58, 61, 62
leftovers 26, 33, 38, 42, 71, 76
Lime loofah 67
lip balm 75
lotion bar 74
lye *see* sodium hydroxide

marbled effect 44, 49, 50, 63, 68
Melon slice 39
melt and pour: method 10, 27
    recipes 32, 33, 34, 38, 39, 43, 62,
    64, 65, 76
mica 65, 66, 71
moisturizing properties 17, 44, 46, 74
mosaic 76
moulds 13, 14, 32, 39, 62,
    64, 65, 67, 72
    releasing soaps from 11

oatmeal 17, 49, 54
oils: base 15, 16, 19
    essential 20, 22–3
    fragrance 20
    infusing 20
    stockists 79
Olive, bran and oatmeal loaf 54
Olive, mango and jojoba 52

Palm kernel with turmeric 57
Passion fruit cake 61
Peppermint cream 63
pH balance 10–11
Pina colada 34
preservatives 15, 18, 23
problems 11, 20
pumice stones 17

re-batching 11, 26
Rosehip and ginger pâté 46
Rosemary sea salt scrub 73

safety precautions 14
saponification 8
    chart 19
scraps *see* leftovers
scrubs 26, 46, 73
Seafood in aspic 43
Seaweed starter 40

seizing 11, 20
sensitive skin 18, 22, 48
setting 9, 11, 27
shampoo bars 17, 23, 52
shortcuts 9
shrinkage 10
silk fibres 18, 66
Silk and shea butter Christmas
    cake 66
skin softening properties 15, 17
Soap balls 69
Soap beads 71
Soap biscuits 69
soda ash, removing 10, 11
sodium hydroxide (caustic soda/lye)
    6–7, 8, 11, 13, 15, 19, 20, 25, 27
    residue in soap 11
    safety when handling 14
    see also cold-process
spices (as colourants) 18, 24, 77
Stained glass slices 65
Strawberry and banana gateau 62
superfatting 11, 15
surface decorations 39, 40, 42, 43, 50,
    62, 69, 71
Sushi 42
Sweethearts 71

Tequila sunrise 32
texture 15, 17, 26, 40, 46, 49
The tip 76
trace 8, 11, 27
    speeding up 9, 15, 17

Vodka on the rocks 38

Walnut and orange loaf 49
water: content of soap 8, 11, 25, 27
    infusing with fragrances 20
    mixing with sodium
      hydroxide 14
    in re-batch 26
wax colourants 25, 77
weights and measures 8, 77
wheatgerm 18
wrapping 28–9, 42